Faith Pray Obey

Faith Pray Obey

40 Keys to Unlocking Spiritual Freedom

Tomeria Jordan

Confident Connotations Publishing

Faith Pray Obey
40 Keys to Unlocking Spiritual Freedom

© 2024. Tomeria Jordan
All Rights Reserved.

All Scripture quotations, unless otherwise indicated, are taken from Bible Gateway (https://www.bible-gateway.com/) who uses the 1987 printing of the King James Version (KJV). The KJV is public domain in the United States.

Confident Connotations Publishing
ISBN (Paperback): 979-8-9887040-2-7
ISBN (Digital Online): 979-8-9887040-3-4
For Worldwide Distribution

First Printing, 2024

This book is dedicated to the body of Christ.
May you always remember who you are and whose you are.

CONTENTS

CONTENTS

Thank you for purchasing and reading this book. My goal is to be a torch to light a flame in your heart and to encourage you to rekindle your fire for God. This book was written by me, Tomeria Jordan, with the guidance of the Holy Spirit and does not contain any content generated by artificial intelligence (AI). Given the state of current events, I want to be sure that whomever is reading this book knows where the content comes from.

My hope is that this 40 day devotional will bless your spirit and encourage you to walk even closer with God, strengthening what is already inside of you. When the trials and tribulations of life come your way, may you be able to withstand the fiery darts of the enemy. I know firsthand what it is like to go through trials. As a matter of fact, I've been through several, so I can proudly acknowledge and appreciate that the reason I am still standing is not because of my own power but because of God's love, grace, and mercy.

Regarding the use of the King James Version (KJV) of the bible for scripture references, this was intentional. Based on historical research, this appears to be the closest copy of the original text in English that is relatively easy to follow. Another reason for this is because some bible versions have started to exclude key scripture references such as Matthew 17:21 which reads "Howbeit this kind goeth not out but by prayer and fasting."

In each chapter, you will find scripture references coupled with personal examples, anecdotes, and/or reflections on the scripture readings. Following each chapter there is a section dedicated to personal reflection. If you happen to be reading this book electronically, use annotations to stop and jot your thoughts. You can also use a personal journal. I've found writing out my thoughts to be very helpful. Not to mention, there are several scriptures in which God reminds the leaders of that time to memorialize what they have experienced as a token of remembrance so they don't forget God's grace is what led them out of certain places. The same holds true for us. So, I encourage you to reflect daily on God's goodness, as well as, what He is showing you.

God has allowed me to write, edit, and release this book in record time and for that I am grateful. What started as an idea on Sunday, April 28th was completed on Wednesday, August 1, 2024. I was able to do so while working full time, traveling, tending to household matters, amongst many other things. In fact, every weekend for 9 weeks I was away from home. But God! To complete this book in 69 days is a testament of faith, praying, and obeying.

You may be wondering when I found time to write. For me, writing before sunrise and work was very productive since by the end of the night I was exhausted. I share this as a reminder to myself, but also as a highlight for you, as a visual representation of what God can do. In fact, Matthew 17:20 reminds us "And Jesus said unto them, Because of your unbelief: for verily I say unto you, If ye have faith as a grain of mustard seed, ye shall say unto this mountain, Remove hence to yonder place; and it shall remove; and nothing shall be impossible unto you." So this is a charge for all believers to be bold and trust God that when we have faith, whatever we pray for, and are committed to submitting to as it relates to being obedient to God's will, it will come to pass.

If you are blessed by this book don't forget to write a review and share it with family and friends because the more reviews that are received, the more individuals we will be able to reach. Writing this book truly blessed my spirit and my hope and prayer is that God will allow it to move and minister to all those in need of his Word for such a time as this. Please remember, this book is not a replacement for God's Word. It is designed to help support you on your journey of faith according to the gifts God has given me.

"For as we have many members in one body, and all members have not the same office: So we, being many, are one body in Christ, and every one members one of another. Having then gifts differing according to the grace that is given to us, whether prophecy, let us prophesy according to the proportion of faith; Or ministry, let us wait on our ministering: or he that teacheth, on teaching; Or he that exhorteth, on exhortation: he that giveth, let him do it with simplicity; he that ruleth, with diligence; he that sheweth mercy, with cheerfulness. Let love be without dissimulation. Abhor that which is evil; cleave to that which is good. Be kindly affectioned one to another with brotherly love; in honour preferring one another; Not slothful in business; fervent in spirit; serving the Lord; Rejoicing in hope; patient in tribulation; continuing instant in prayer; Distributing to the necessity of saints; given to hospitality." Romans 12:4-13 KJV

I feel grateful to have gifts that allow me to share my life experience in hopes of encouraging others. It reminds me of 1 Corinthians 3:6-8 which reads "So then neither is he that planteth any thing, neither he that watereth; but God that giveth the increase. Now he that planteth and he that watereth are one: and every man shall receive his own reward according to his own labour."

In closing, my hope is that your faith will increase as you walk closer with God, your prayer life will improve, your ability to hear and obey

God will grow, and you will be able to slay any giants that you face. Remember, God always gets it right. It is time to lift up your head and shine your light.

Sincerely,

Tomeria Jordan

As you read this devotional, below are some key items to reflect on and document as part of your journey. The devotional pages which follow each chapter have been left open to allow you the freedom to express yourself in the manner that fits you best. For example, it could be written, it could be a drawing, or it could be something else. This is how God wants us to come to Him. Free to be who He created us to be.

1. **Gratitude: Today, I'm grateful for...**
   Use this space to highlight what you are grateful for. Every day is a gift so we will start each day with thanksgiving.

2. **Dreams: I had a dream...**
   Dreams are powerful and are often how God communicates with His children. When we have open doors, meaning we have not repented for our shortcomings, the enemy can choke out our ability to hear God's instruction. Use this space to document what you recall so that you can ask the Holy Spirit to show you what it means. You can also use this space to document your vision based on what you believe will happen today, this week, or in the future.

3. **Mediate: Today, I'm meditating on...**
   Use this section to highlight scriptures that you would like to meditate on. Joshua 1:8 reminds us "This book of the law shall not depart out of thy mouth; but thou shalt meditate therein day and night, that thou mayest observe to do according to all that

is written therein: for then thou shalt make thy way prosperous, and then thou shalt have good success."

4. **Daily Devotion**

Use this space to document what God is showing you. This will be important for you as you journey through these next 40 days because to see God show up and move is a mighty powerful thing. Trust me, God has seen me through and I do not doubt that he won't show up for you. So whether that is showing you where you have erred, or giving you grace for the place you are in, I've learned over time that when you are open to God, God will be open to you. Matthew 7:7-8 reminds us to "Ask, and it shall be given you; seek, and ye shall find; knock, and it shall be opened unto you: For every one that asketh receiveth; and he that seeketh findeth; and to him that knocketh it shall be opened."

First and foremost giving all glory to God for his grace and mercy. I felt led to write this book to help individuals break free from the chains that bind them in early 2024. As a result, I drafted a prototype only for the draft to be unsaved and hence deleted.

On Sunday, April 28, 2024, I woke up before sunrise and the devotional came to mind again but with urgency. As a result, I sprang into action, outlining the 40-day journey while listening to the book of Exodus via my Bible app. I share this because others need to know that this book was written by faith, through a continuous prayer conversation with God, and obedience to what I felt led to do.

I believed that God could and would help me write this book in record time and it is now in our hands. One thing is for certain, and two things are for sure, when God gets ready to move there is nothing that can shut the door.

Let's get into it!

One

Day 1 - Blessed Yet Bound

> "And the children of Israel were fruitful, and increased abundantly, and multiplied, and waxed exceeding mighty; and the land was filled with them." Exodus 1:7 KJV

Blessed Yet Bound

In the first book of Exodus it is chronicled how fruitful and abundant the children of Israel were in the land of Egypt. When a new ruler came into power, Pharaoh, he took note of how abundant the descendants were and decided in his heart and professed with his mouth that the children of Israel needed to be stopped lest they multiply and destroy the Egyptians in the future. While Pharaoh did not have evidence of this, he believed it to be true and that is why he chose to enslave the children of Israel as chronicled in Exodus 1.

"And the children of Israel were fruitful, and increased abundantly, and multiplied, and waxed exceeding mighty; and the land was filled with them. Now there arose up a new king over Egypt, which knew not Joseph. And he said unto his people, Behold, the people of the children of Israel are more and mightier than we: Come on, let us deal wisely with them; lest they multiply, and it come to pass, that, when there falleth out any war, they join also unto our enemies, and fight against us, and so get them up out of the land. Therefore they did set over them taskmasters to afflict them with their burdens. And they built for Pharaoh treasure cities, Pithom and Raamses. But the more they afflicted them, the more they multiplied and grew. And they were grieved because of the children of Israel. And the Egyptians made the children of Israel to serve with rigour: And they made their lives bitter with hard bondage, in morter, and in brick, and in all manner of service in the field: all their service, wherein they made them serve, was with rigour." Exodus 1: 7-14 KJV

The children of Israel had God's favor yet they found themselves bound by Pharaoh's belief that their favor wasn't fair and that one day they would grow into a mighty army and destroy the Egyptians. The scripture reminds us that in spite of being afflicted, they multiplied and grew. This message isn't only about the children of Israel, it is also a great reminder for me and you. Similar to the children of Israel, some of us may find ourselves in predicaments where someone who does not know us passes a judgment because we have favor. So it is quite possible to be blessed in the midst of the "mess."

The enemy, Satan, is waging war against the body of Christ (Revelation 12). Because we are blessed, the enemy sends people, situations, and circumstances to try to keep us bound. This devotional was written in response to the bondage Satan hopes to keep us in. When we acknowledge where we are, we can see where we are going, and we can take the necessary steps in faith to get free.

Gratitude: Today, I'm grateful for...
Every day is a gift! Use this space to reflect on what you are thankful for.

Dreams: I had a dream...
Use this space to document what you recall from your dreams so that you can ask the Holy Spirit to show you what it means. You can also use this space to document your vision based on what you believe will happen today, this week, or in the future.

Mediate: Today, I'm meditating on...
Use this section to highlight scriptures that you would like to meditate on.

Daily Devotion
Use this space to document what God is showing you as you navigate this 40-day journey.

Two

Day 2 - Bruised Not Broken

"For God, who commanded the light to shine out of darkness, hath shined in our hearts, to give the light of the knowledge of the glory of God in the face of Jesus Christ. But we have this treasure in earthen vessels, that the excellency of the power may be of God, and not of us. We are troubled on every side, yet not distressed; we are perplexed, but not in despair; Persecuted, but not forsaken; cast down, but not destroyed;" 2 Corinthians 4: 6-9 KJV

Bruised Not Broken

Ironically, in the course of writing this journal, I slipped and injured my big toe on my left foot. I was walking to an event to celebrate my eldest sister's birthday and slid across a manhole cover on a downtown street. Shortly after sliding, I noticed that my toe, which was hit by the metal framing, started to swell. This pain felt all too familiar since in 2018 I fell down the stairs while pregnant and both feet swelled within 2 hours. What I learned after that fall was that I had broken my big toe on my left foot and sprained my right ankle. In spite of the all too familiar feeling resurfacing, I decided to pray. The injury occurred around 2PM on Saturday, April 27, 2024 and I prayed shortly thereafter that in spite of what it looks like that I would be able to walk on my left foot without incident and that my big toe wouldn't be broken seeing as though I needed to travel back home and I didn't have anyone to help drive. Fast forward to today, April 30, 2024 at 6:09PM EST, which is when I'm writing this excerpt, I can declare that my toe is not broken. Much like in my situation, the children of Israel were bruised by their affliction yet they weren't broken because of God's grace and mercy.

"So they put slave masters over them to oppress them with forced labor, and they built Pithom and Rameses as store cities for Pharaoh. But the more they were oppressed, the more they multiplied and spread; so the Egyptians came to dread the Israelites." Exodus 1:11-12 KJV

Today, you may find yourself in a situation where you've been bruised and in some cases battered by what you've been through as a result of the storms we face in life. In spite of the trials you may be facing, my hope is that today's devotional serves as a reminder that you are not broken. You still function just the same. As a result, ask

God in faith for more grace, mercy, and favor as you move forward with great expectation that there is something greater waiting for you on the other side of the difficulties you face.

Gratitude: Today, I'm grateful for...
Every day is a gift! Use this space to reflect on what you are thankful for.

Dreams: I had a dream...
Use this space to document what you recall from your dreams so that you can ask the Holy Spirit to show you what it means. You can also use this space to document your vision based on what you believe will happen today, this week, or in the future.

Mediate: Today, I'm meditating on...

Use this section to highlight scriptures that you would like to meditate on.

Daily Devotion

Use this space to document what God is showing you as you navigate this 40-day journey.

Three

Day 3 - A Bitter Cup

"And the king of Egypt spake to the Hebrew midwives, of which the name of the one was Shiphrah, and the name of the other Puah: and he said, When ye do the office of a midwife to the Hebrew women, and see them upon the stools; if it be a son, then ye shall kill him: but if it be a daughter, then she shall live. But the midwives feared God, and did not as the king of Egypt commanded them, but saved the men children alive. And the king of Egypt called for the midwives, and said unto them, Why have ye done this thing, and have saved the men children alive? And the midwives said unto Pharaoh, Because the Hebrew women are not as the Egyptian women; for they are lively, and are delivered ere the midwives come in unto them. Therefore God dealt well with the midwives: and the people multiplied, and waxed very mighty. And it came to pass, because the midwives feared God, that he made them houses." Exodus 1:15-21 KJV

A Bitter Cup

I heard a wise woman by the name of Jaye Wilson say her late grand-mother used to tell her " you have to go through to get through" and that always stuck with me from the day she said it as a guest on the Confidence Restored Podcast. Episode 44 was all about resilience as we chronicled our birthing experiences and her business Melinated Moms. During that episode I recall the fact that I started the Confidence Re-stored podcast after going through a month-long miscarriage. February 17, 2020 amid the start of the Covid-19 pandemic I had a dilation and curettage also known as a D&C because my husband and I were told the week before that our baby no longer had a heartbeat. Within a week, I had a fever and began bleeding again. I was asked to come back to my OBGYN to be evaluated only for them to find that in spite of the sur-gery I still had a lot of tissue left. Given the maternal health crisis in the United States, this was a big deal, especially as a woman of color who by statistics are more than 3x as likely to die as a result of pregnancy related complications. In my case, I know it was nothing but God's grace and mercy that kept me alive. While I didn't understand then why I was going through what I went through, I now believe that it was to catapult me into my destiny. My faith has certainly increased and my mission to share my testimony to help others get free motivates me.

So regarding the miscarriage, how did things end? On March 27, 2020 I received a phone call from my medical provider. After 13 miscarriage (also referred to as abortion) pills, multiple sonograms, and several pelvic exams, they told me that the results were all clear. Considering when this process started, February 17th, I recognize and appreciate that I am a miracle walking. Things could have certainly taken a drastic turn given the retained products of conception, but God!

I truly believe that my life isn't a mistake and I know yours isn't either. So I encourage you to reflect on the moments and miracles that you've experienced and how it has shaped you into the person that you are. Consider the children of Israel in Exodus 1 verses 15-21.

"And the king of Egypt spake to the Hebrew midwives, of which the name of the one was Shiphrah, and the name of the other Puah: and he said, When ye do the office of a midwife to the Hebrew women, and see them upon the stools; if it be a son, then ye shall kill him: but if it be a daughter, then she shall live. But the midwives feared God, and did not as the king of Egypt commanded them, but saved the men children alive. And the king of Egypt called for the midwives, and said unto them, Why have ye done this thing, and have saved the men children alive? And the midwives said unto Pharaoh, Because the Hebrew women are not as the Egyptian women; for they are lively, and are delivered ere the midwives come in unto them. Therefore God dealt well with the midwives: and the people multiplied, and waxed very mighty. And it came to pass, because the midwives feared God, that he made them houses." Exodus 1:15-21 KJV

You may have a bitter cup today but that doesn't mean you can't or will not have a bountiful cup tomorrow.

Gratitude: Today, I'm grateful for...
Every day is a gift! Use this space to reflect on what you are thankful for.

Dreams: I had a dream...
Use this space to document what you recall from your dreams so that you can ask the Holy Spirit to show you what it means. You can also use this space to document your vision based on what you believe will happen today, this week, or in the future.

Mediate: Today, I'm meditating on...
Use this section to highlight scriptures that you would like to meditate on.

Daily Devotion
Use this space to document what God is showing you as you navigate this 40-day journey.

Four

Day 4 - No Longer Hidden

"And when she could not longer hide him, she took for him an ark of bulrushes, and daubed it with slime and with pitch, and put the child therein; and she laid it in the flags by the river's brink. And his sister stood afar off, to wit what would be done to him. And the daughter of Pharaoh came down to wash herself at the river; and her maidens walked along by the river's side; and when she saw the ark among the flags, she sent her maid to fetch it. And when she had opened it, she saw the child: and, behold, the babe wept. And she had compassion on him, and said, This is one of the Hebrews' children." Exodus 2:3-6 KJV

No Longer Hidden

Much like in the book of Exodus, sometimes God hides us, because he knows what we have inside, and he wants to protect us from the enemy's plans and plots. Much like in Exodus 2 verses 3 through 6, it chronicles the fact that Moses, a Hebrew child, was born and hidden by his mother because she saw that "he was a goodly child." While Moses was given the name Moses by Pharaoh's daughter due to the fact that he was drawn out of the water, his birth speaks volumes about his life being divinely protected.

"And the woman conceived, and bare a son: and when she saw him that he was a goodly child, she hid him three months. And when she could not longer hide him, she took for him an ark of bulrushes, and daubed it with slime and with pitch, and put the child therein; and she laid it in the flags by the river's brink. And his sister stood afar off, to wit what would be done to him. And the daughter of Pharaoh came down to wash herself at the river; and her maidens walked along by the river's side; and when she saw the ark among the flags, she sent her maid to fetch it. And when she had opened it, she saw the child: and, behold, the babe wept. And she had compassion on him, and said, This is one of the Hebrews' children. Then said his sister to Pharaoh's daughter, Shall I go and call to thee a nurse of the Hebrew women, that she may nurse the child for thee? And Pharaoh's daughter said to her, Go. And the maid went and called the child's mother. And Pharaoh's daughter said unto her, Take this child away, and nurse it for me, and I will give thee thy wages. And the women took the child, and nursed it. And the child grew, and she brought him unto Pharaoh's daughter, and he became her son. And she called his name Moses: and she said, Because I drew him out of the water." Exodus 2:3-10 KJV

Moses went from being hidden to being protected in the kingdom of the king that requested in Exodus 1 that all Hebrew male children be destroyed. This example is powerful and speaks to the fact that sometimes when we are hidden it's not God's denial, it's His protection. In fact, when you think of life, there are many things that society deems valuable that are hidden. For instance, diamonds, pearls, and the like. They require work to reach.

Today, be encouraged in knowing that if you are experiencing a period of drought or perhaps shielding fiery darts from the enemy, remember that God sometimes covers us in an ark to keep us safe from further harm so that we can carry out his will at an appointed time.

Daily Devotion (Day 4)

Gratitude: Today, I'm grateful for...
Every day is a gift! Use this space to reflect on what you are thankful for.

Dreams: I had a dream...
Use this space to document what you recall from your dreams so that you can ask the Holy Spirit to show you what it means. You can also use this space to document your vision based on what you believe will happen today, this week, or in the future.

Mediate: Today, I'm meditating on...
Use this section to highlight scriptures that you would like to meditate on.

Daily Devotion
Use this space to document what God is showing you as you navigate this 40-day journey.

Five

Day 5 - Drawn Out

"And the daughter of Pharaoh came down to wash herself at the river; and her maidens walked along by the river's side; and when she saw the ark among the flags, she sent her maid to fetch it. And when she had opened it, she saw the child: and, behold, the babe wept. And she had compassion on him, and said, This is one of the Hebrews' children. Then said his sister to Pharaoh's daughter, Shall I go and call to thee a nurse of the Hebrew women, that she may nurse the child for thee? And Pharaoh's daughter said to her, Go. And the maid went and called the child's mother. And Pharaoh's daughter said unto her, Take this child away, and nurse it for me, and I will give thee thy wages. And the woman took the child, and nursed it. And the child grew, and she brought him unto Pharaoh's daughter, and he became her son. And she called his name Moses: and she said, Because I drew him out of the water." Exodus 2:5-10 KJV

Drawn Out

Today we're continuing on in the story of Moses. After Moses was found in the water, Pharaoh's daughter told her maid to draw him out and find his mother to nurse him. Once he was strengthened, Pharaoh's daughter raised him as her own child. As you can imagine, being raised in Pharaoh's house, Moses had favor. Everything that Moses' needed we can reasonably presume he had in spite of being a Hebrew.

There may be times in your life where you feel out of place yet that doesn't mean that you cannot be showered by God's grace. I like to call what Moses experienced a divine delay because there was a period of time in which he was hidden yet in due time his purpose was revealed.

This reminds me of the story of Esther in which she was raised and advised by her cousin and guardian Mordecai to not tell anyone that she was a Jew when she was brought into the palace to be purified and prepared to meet the king as part of his search for a new wife (Esther 2). After finding favor with the king, Esther was crowned yet when it came time for her to share her heritage with her husband to save the Jewish people, Esther had some tough decisions to make.

"Again Esther spake unto Hatach, and gave him commandment unto Mordecai; All the king's servants, and the people of the king's provinces, do know, that whosoever, whether man or women, shall come unto the king into the inner court, who is not called, there is one law of his to put him to death, except such to whom the king shall hold out the golden sceptre, that he may live: but I have not been called to come in unto the king these thirty days. And they told to Mordecai Esther's words. Then Mordecai commanded to answer Esther, Think not with thyself that thou shalt escape in the king's house, more than all the Jews. For if thou altogether holdest thy peace at this time, then shall there enlargement and deliverance arise to the Jews from another place; but thou and thy father's house shall be destroyed: and who knoweth whether thou art come to the kingdom for such a time as this? Then Esther bade them return Mordecai this answer, Go, gather together all the Jews that are present in Shushan, and fast ye for me, and neither eat nor drink three days, night or day: I also and my maidens will fast likewise; and so will I go in unto the king, which is not according to the law: and if I perish, I perish. So Mordecai went his way, and did according to all that Esther had commanded him." Esther 4:10-17 KJV

So the reminder here is to think about where you've been planted. Perhaps you've been planted on purpose so you can grow in the interim and when the time comes for you to reveal who you are, you will be prepared. Having more experiences, knowledge, and more wisdom to walk in the area in which you have been called.

Often times in society we try to fit in but there are times where you've been appointed to stand out. Remember, where you are now doesn't mean that is where you always have to be and you can purpose in your heart that "regardless of what I see, I can trust that God is working some things out for me."

Daily Devotion (Day 5)

Gratitude: Today, I'm grateful for...
Every day is a gift! Use this space to reflect on what you are thankful for.

Dreams: I had a dream...
Use this space to document what you recall from your dreams so that you can ask the Holy Spirit to show you what it means. You can also use this space to document your vision based on what you believe will happen today, this week, or in the future.

Mediate: Today, I'm meditating on...
Use this section to highlight scriptures that you would like to meditate on.

Daily Devotion
Use this space to document what God is showing you as you navigate this 40-day journey.

Six

Day 6 - Fallen Off

"And it came to pass in those days, when Moses was grown, that he went out unto his brethren, and looked on their burdens: and he spied an Egyptian smiting an Hebrew, one of his brethren. And he looked this way and that way, and when he saw that there was no man, he slew the Egyptian, and hid him in the sand. And when he went out the second day, behold, two men of the Hebrews strove together: and he said to him that did the wrong, Wherefore smitest thou thy fellow? And he said, Who made thee a prince and a judge over us? intendest thou to kill me, as thou killedst the Egyptian? And Moses feared, and said, Surely this thing is known. Now when Pharaoh heard this thing, he sought to slay Moses. But Moses fled from the face of Pharaoh, and dwelt in the land of Midian: and he sat down by a well."
Exodus 2:11-15 KJV

Fallen Off

In Exodus 2 we see that Moses acted out of anger after witnessing the mistreatment of his brethren. When we think about our own lives there may be situations and circumstances where we have allowed other people or experiences to get us off track. As a result, we tend to fall back from God because of our life decisions. Some of this can be attributed to fear of the consequences we believe are coming our way. Other times it's because of the shame that is associated with our actions.

Today, I want to encourage and let you know that it may feel natural to run and hide; however, that is the enemy's hope. When we hide, we don't allow God to utilize what we may have experienced as a testimony to his grace and mercy which often results in others joining the body of Christ.

In Revelation 12:10, we are reminded that "...Now is come salvation, and strength, and the kingdom of our God, and the power of his Christ: for the accuser of our brethren is cast down, which accused them before our God day and night." I have often said, we cannot heal what is not revealed. While God knows all, he gives us free will regarding repentance as well as our decision to obey, harken to the Word, and do things God's way. When we let Satan go to God on our behalf, we rob ourselves of the freedom that comes with knowing Christ. This doesn't mean we get a pass to keep on sinning, it just means that we are willing to humble ourselves, repent, and accept God's correction over the condemnation we may be used to feeling.

I encourage you to think about any transgressions you may be hiding so that you can repent to God, renounce the behavior, and replace it with the gift God has given you.

Daily Devotion (Day 6)

Gratitude: Today, I'm grateful for...
Every day is a gift! Use this space to reflect on what you are thankful for.

Dreams: I had a dream...
Use this space to document what you recall from your dreams so that you can ask the Holy Spirit to show you what it means. You can also use this space to document your vision based on what you believe will happen today, this week, or in the future.

Mediate: Today, I'm meditating on...
Use this section to highlight scriptures that you would like to meditate on.

Daily Devotion
Use this space to document what God is showing you as you navigate this 40-day journey.

Seven

Day 7 - Stranger in a Strange Land

" "And they said, An Egyptian delivered us out of the hand "" of the shepherds, and also drew water enough for us, and watered the flock. And he said unto his daughters, And where is he? why is it that ye have left the man? call him, that he may eat bread. And Moses was content to dwell with the man: and he gave Moses Zipporah his daughter. And she bare him a son, and he called his name Gershom: for he said, I have been a stranger in a strange land." Exodus 2:19-22 KJV

Stranger in a Strange Land

While sojourning, Moses encountered Midian's daughters by a well and helped them. Because he freely supported them without expectation, their Father, Reuel, asked his daughters to bring Moses back to their home so that he could "eat bread."

"Now the priest of Midian had seven daughters: and they came and drew water, and filled the troughs to water their father's flock. And the shepherds came and drove them away: but Moses stood up and helped them, and watered their flock. And when they came to Reuel their father, he said, How is it that ye are come so soon to day. And they said, An Egyptian delivered us out of the hand of the shepherds, and also drew water enough for us, and watered the flock. And he said unto his daughters, And where is he? why is it that ye have left the man? call him, that he may eat bread. And Moses was content to dwell with the man: and he gave Moses Zipporah his daughter. And she bare him a son, and he called his name Gershom: for he said, I have been a stranger in a strange land. And it came to pass in process of time, that the king of Egypt died: and the children of Israel sighed by reason of the bondage, and they cried, and their cry came up unto God by reason of the bondage. And God heard their groaning, and God remembered his covenant with Abraham, with Isaac, and with Jacob. And God looked upon the children of Israel, and God had respect unto them." Exodus 2:16-25 KJV

So as we can see in Exodus 2, Moses and Zipporah had a son whose name meant "stranger in a strange land." While Moses was there, God heard the cry of his brethren back in Egypt after the king died and he had respect upon the people. In Exodus 3, Moses was keeping the flock of Jethro, his father in law, the priest of Midian, when an angel of the

Lord appeared unto him in a flame of fire from a nearby bush. So in spite of the mistake Moses made many years prior, God still called to him after remembering the covenant with his forefathers.

When we look back over Moses' journey thus far there are a series of highs and lows. So let's think about it at a high-level.

1. Moses was hidden for 3 months as a newborn to save his life.
2. Moses was returned to his mother to gain strength before being returned to Pharaoh's daughter.
3. Moses was raised in the palace to give him experience for his future position.
4. Moses sinned out of anger, killed an Egyptian, and fled to a foreign land.
5. In Exodus 2, we find that Moses helped strangers and received blessings from their Father.

In spite of being a stranger in a strange land due to life decisions and in many cases circumstances, Moses still had favor. This example is a testament to the fact that God's grace and mercy covers us and it also highlights how God can send blessings through the most unlikely sources. When you think about your own life and journey up until this point, can you think of any life situations in which you were blessed in an unlikely situation or a "strange land?"

Daily Devotion (Day 7)

Gratitude: Today, I'm grateful for...
Every day is a gift! Use this space to reflect on what you are thankful for.

Dreams: I had a dream...
Use this space to document what you recall from your dreams so that you can ask the Holy Spirit to show you what it means. You can also use this space to document your vision based on what you believe will happen today, this week, or in the future.

Mediate: Today, I'm meditating on...
Use this section to highlight scriptures that you would like to meditate on.

Daily Devotion
Use this space to document what God is showing you as you navigate this 40-day journey.

Eight

Day 8 - Hear This

"And when the LORD saw that he turned aside to see, God called unto him out of the midst of the bush, and said, Moses, Moses. And he said, Here am I. And he said, Draw not nigh hither: put off thy shoes from off thy feet, for the place whereon thou standest is holy ground. Moreover he said, I am the God of thy father, the God of Abraham, the God of Isaac, and the God of Jacob. And Moses hid his face; for he was afraid to look upon God. And the LORD said, I have surely seen the affliction of my people which are in Egypt, and have heard their cry by reason of their taskmasters; for I know their sorrows; and I am come down to deliver them out of the hand of the Egyptians, and to bring them up out of that land unto a good land and a large, unto a land flowing with milk and honey; unto the place of the Canaanites, and the Hittites, and the Amorites, and the Perizzites, and the Hivites, and the Jebusites. Now therefore, behold, the cry of the children of Israel is come unto me: and I have also seen the oppression wherewith the Egyptians oppress them. Come now therefore, and I will send thee unto Pharaoh, that thou mayest bring forth my people the children of Israel out of Egypt." Exodus 3:4-10 KJV

Hear This

Our Father which art is heaven is calling us today much like he called Moses. Every day we wake up is a gift from God and can be considered a call. If you have been using social media, or watching the news, you have likely witnessed people sharing their testimonies and crediting Jesus Christ for their success. While this isn't new, it speaks to the fact that no matter where we are, what job we have, or what goals we accomplish the only reason we have breath in our body is because our creator said so.

While writing this book I had a very scary encounter. This situation, while not uncommon for a lot of drivers, forced me to take a step back and consider why I've been blessed to still exist when so many situations around us can be amiss. On Saturday, May 4th while driving home to visit family before heading to a celebration of life/homegoing service I was on interstate 95 heading southbound when a driver came out of nowhere speeding up behind my vehicle. I could see the driver in the rear-view mirror driving erratically and they had recently swerved from behind another vehicle and abruptly moved in front of them. As I saw them approaching my body tensed up because there was no where for me to go. When I started to move left, they went left, I tried to move right, they went right, and steadily the gap between our vehicles was closing. The speed limit was 70 MPH and I was driving between 60 and 70MPH and judging from how quickly they approached one could presume they were driving between 80 and 90 MPH. As a result I couldn't accurately judge what move I should make, so...I stayed in my lane.

Within seconds the driver was nearing the rear bumper of my vehicle and to God be the glory the driver swerved over just in time, barely missing my vehicle. I immediately began to praise God because I know it was only through God's grace and mercy that my life was preserved in that moment. One wrong move could have resulted in a catastrophic outcome.

In a nutshell, I did not know what the other driver's intention was. When we think about life, that is sometimes how the enemy approaches us and it throws us off track. Satan comes in quickly causing us to look back, get distracted, and sometimes worse. Even in spite of the unexpected circumstances we can trust God that he can protect us when we don't know which way to move.

I shared the aforementioned example because much like Moses, I noticed the other vehicle yet I couldn't afford to lose focus. Losing focus in that moment would have stopped me from driving forward. When Moses saw the burning bush he knew he needed to move forward yet at that moment he didn't know how.

In the moments chronicled above, and in this moment, God is speaking. Think about what God has been speaking to your heart. For me, I believe the message is to trust God wholeheartedly regardless of what I see. For someone else it may be a reminder to be still although you see the enemy approaching fast and furiously. In spite of what we see in the natural, we can have faith that God is and will take care of us much like he heard the cries of his children in Exodus 3.

Daily Devotion (Day 8)

Gratitude: Today, I'm grateful for...
Every day is a gift! Use this space to reflect on what you are thankful for.

Dreams: I had a dream...
Use this space to document what you recall from your dreams so that you can ask the Holy Spirit to show you what it means. You can also use this space to document your vision based on what you believe will happen today, this week, or in the future.

Mediate: Today, I'm meditating on...

Use this section to highlight scriptures that you would like to meditate on.

Daily Devotion

Use this space to document what God is showing you as you navigate this 40-day journey.

Nine

Day 9 - Unqualified

"And Moses said unto God, Who am I, that I should go unto Pharaoh, and that I should bring forth the children of Israel out of Egypt?" Exodus 3:11 KJV

Unqualified

Revisiting the topic of qualifications, let's explore the definition of being unqualified. Many sources have defined being unqualified as not fit for or lacking the necessary qualifications through training, skills, or experience to carry out a particular task. Synonyms include words like "unfit", or "incompetent." When we think about Moses' selection, he most certainly provided reasons that he believed he was not the right person for the job, but God.

"And Moses said unto the Lord, O my Lord, I am not eloquent, neither heretofore, nor since thou hast spoken unto thy servant: but I am slow of speech, and of a slow tongue. And the Lord said unto him, Who hath made man's mouth? or who maketh the dumb, or deaf, or the seeing, or the blind? have not I the Lord? Now therefore go, and I will be with thy mouth, and teach thee what thou shalt say. And he said, O my Lord, send, I pray thee, by the hand of him whom thou wilt send. And the anger of the Lord was kindled against Moses, and he said, Is not Aaron the Levite thy brother? I know that he can speak well. And also, behold, he cometh forth to meet thee: and when he seeth thee, he will be glad in his heart. And thou shalt speak unto him, and put words in his mouth: and I will be with thy mouth, and with his mouth, and will teach you what ye shall do. And he shall be thy spokesman unto the people: and he shall be, even he shall be to thee instead of a mouth, and thou shalt be to him instead of God. And thou shalt take this rod in thine hand, wherewith thou shalt do signs." Exodus 3:10-17 KJV

In spite of what God said, Moses responded with excuses. He knew what God was asking him to do sounded nearly impossible especially given the fact that Moses hadn't returned to Egypt in the past because of his personal sin against the Egyptian taskmaster. God didn't care about his excuses because he knew that his grace was sufficient yet he permitted Moses' brother Aaron to speak on his behalf with the expectation that Moses would perform the signs.

For some of us, we believe in our heart that God has called us to do something yet because of society's standards or our own doubts and disbelief we have decided that we are unqualified to carry out God's divine purpose for our lives. May Moses' example demonstrate the need for faith and remind us that we shouldn't refer to ourselves as unqualified when God qualifies us through his power, grace, and mercy.

Daily Devotion (Day 9)

Gratitude: Today, I'm grateful for...
Every day is a gift! Use this space to reflect on what you are thankful for.

Dreams: I had a dream...
Use this space to document what you recall from your dreams so that you can ask the Holy Spirit to show you what it means. You can also use this space to document your vision based on what you believe will happen today, this week, or in the future.

Mediate: Today, I'm meditating on...
Use this section to highlight scriptures that you would like to meditate on.

Daily Devotion
Use this space to document what God is showing you as you navigate this 40-day journey.

Ten

Day 10 - Qualified by God

"And he said, Certainly I will be with thee; and this shall be a token unto thee, that I have sent thee: When thou hast brought forth the people out of Egypt, ye shall serve God upon this mountain." Exodus 3:12 KJV

Qualified by God

What does it mean to be qualified by God? Being qualified by God means that we are able to move forward in achieving God's will for our life through God's unmerited favor which is also called grace. God will allow us to do more, go further, and reach more people not by our own hands but by his supernatural power bestowed upon us. For instance, Jeremiah was called to be a prophet of God not in his own strength but by God's power. In fact Jeremiah was called before he was born for the position that he would later fulfill.

"Before I formed thee in the belly I knew thee; and before thou camest forth out of the womb I sanctified thee, and I ordained thee a prophet unto the nations. Then said I, Ah, Lord God! behold, I cannot speak: for I am a child. But the Lord said unto me, Say not, I am a child: for thou shalt go to all that I shall send thee, and whatsoever I command thee thou shalt speak. Be not afraid of their faces: for I am with thee to deliver thee, saith the Lord. Then the Lord put forth his hand, and touched my mouth. And the Lord said unto me, Behold, I have put my words in thy mouth. See, I have this day set thee over the nations and over the kingdoms, to root out, and to pull down, and to destroy, and to throw down, to build, and to plant." Jeremiah 1:5-10 KJV

You may feel like you are not worthy of the gift you have received yet we learned from Moses and Jeremiah's testimonies that God will do what he said he will do. In both scenarios, God gave them the words, wisdom, and abilities yet they also had to be obedient to God's call and direction.

Today, ask God to show you through the power of the Holy Spirit what he wants you to see regarding your destiny.

Daily Devotion (Day 10)

Gratitude: Today, I'm grateful for...

Every day is a gift! Use this space to reflect on what you are thankful for.

Dreams: I had a dream...

Use this space to document what you recall from your dreams so that you can ask the Holy Spirit to show you what it means. You can also use this space to document your vision based on what you believe will happen today, this week, or in the future.

Mediate: Today, I'm meditating on...
Use this section to highlight scriptures that you would like to meditate on.

Daily Devotion
Use this space to document what God is showing you as you navigate this 40-day journey.

Eleven

Day 11 - Called

"And Moses said unto God, Behold, when I come unto the children of Israel, and shall say unto them, The God of your fathers hath sent me unto you; and they shall say to me, What is his name? what shall I say unto them? And God said unto Moses, I AM THAT I AM: and he said, Thus shalt thou say unto the children of Israel, I AM hath sent me unto you. And God said moreover unto Moses, Thus shalt thou say unto the children of Israel, The LORD God of your fathers, the God of Abraham, the God of Isaac, and the God of Jacob, hath sent me unto you: this is my name for ever, and this is my memorial unto all generations." Exodus 3:13-15 KJV

Called

When you feel like you are being called by God, reflect on how that feels and what you have experienced. In thinking about this experience ask yourself what is the alternative? I can personally attest to the fact that there have been times where I would like to get a message out and I simply cannot rest until it is complete. There have also been times where I felt led to do something that may seem simple to others but I later learn that it is profound to God because it comes in the form of an answered prayer for someone else.

Let me give you a more practical example. I was standing in church service and subconsciously thought to give the person to my right $20. I wrestled with the thought, meaning, I wondered if it was me or if it was God. I was also afraid that doing so could be considered offensive since they hadn't asked and/or alluded to needing any money. Eventually I thought to myself, what is the harm in doing so? If it is God, I've been obedient, and if it's not God, I've been a blessing. Unbeknownst to me, the individual drove to church knowing they didn't have enough money nor gas to make it home. They told me thank you and shared the fact that this $20 blessing was an answered prayer.

I personally have had several situations and encounters like this which remind me that God will ask us to do things that may not seem like a big deal to some yet to others it could literally be a turning point in their relationship and walk with God.

"Then shall the King say unto them on his right hand, Come, ye blessed of my Father, inherit the kingdom prepared for you from the foundation of the world: For I was an hungred, and ye gave me meat: I was thirsty, and ye gave me drink: I was a stranger, and ye took me in: Naked, and ye clothed me: I was sick, and ye visited me: I was in prison, and ye came unto me. Then shall the righteous answer him, saying, Lord, when saw we thee an hungred, and fed thee? or thirsty, and gave thee drink? When saw we thee a stranger, and took thee in? or naked, and clothed thee? Or when saw we thee sick, or in prison, and came unto thee? And the King shall answer and say unto them, Verily I say unto you, Inasmuch as ye have done it unto one of the least of these my brethren, ye have done it unto me." Matthew 25:34-40 KJV

Being called to do anything by definition means that someone is crying out or attempting to attract someone's attention. God wants to get your attention today to let you know that what you may call small may mean more to the Kingdom of God because you are "called." In fact, Matthew 22:14 reminds us "For many are called, but few are chosen."

Daily Devotion (Day 11)

Gratitude: Today, I'm grateful for...
Every day is a gift! Use this space to reflect on what you are thankful for.

Dreams: I had a dream...
Use this space to document what you recall from your dreams so that you can ask the Holy Spirit to show you what it means. You can also use this space to document your vision based on what you believe will happen today, this week, or in the future.

Mediate: Today, I'm meditating on...

Use this section to highlight scriptures that you would like to meditate on.

Daily Devotion

Use this space to document what God is showing you as you navigate this 40-day journey.

Twelve

Day 12 - God's Got a Message

“ "Go, and gather the elders of Israel together, and say unto ”
them, The Lord God of your fathers, the God of Abraham,
of Isaac, and of Jacob, appeared unto me, saying, I have
surely visited you, and seen that which is done to you in
Egypt: And I have said, I will bring you up out of the affliction
of Egypt unto the land of the Canaanites, and the Hittites,
and the Amorites, and the Perizzites, and the Hivites, and
the Jebusites, unto a land flowing with milk and honey. And
they shall hearken to thy voice: and thou shalt come, thou
and the elders of Israel, unto the king of Egypt, and ye shall
say unto him, The Lord God of the Hebrews hath met with
us: and now let us go, we beseech thee, three days' journey
into the wilderness, that we may sacrifice to the Lord our
God. And I am sure that the king of Egypt will not let you
go, no, not by a mighty hand. And I will stretch out my hand,
and smite Egypt with all my wonders which I will do in the
midst thereof: and after that he will let you go. And I will
give this people favour in the sight of the Egyptians: and it
shall come to pass, that, when ye go, ye shall not go empty."
Exodus 3:18-21 KJV

God's Got a Message

Life is full of ups and downs but when God gives you or your ancestors a promise you can believe it will come to pass. In Exodus 3:21 God sent a very powerful message to the children of Israel "And I will give this people favour in the sight of the Egyptians: and it shall come to pass, that, when ye go, ye shall not go empty." Sometimes when we hear God's message we have a hard time believing it because of what we see in the natural yet the Word reminds us in Matthew 17:20 that if we have the faith of a mustard seed we can move mountains. Nothing shall be impossible to us but we must first believe.

When I was wondering if I should take a new job in 2013 I faced a lot of internal turmoil because I would need to leave a place where I was comfortable. I had just recently had a lot of work done to my home and I had practically decided in my heart that if I didn't get the new job it would be okay because I proactively shifted some other things around which would allow me to just enjoy where I was. Well, a job I applied for in March was offered to me in May. As I grappled with this decision to stay where I was comfortable or move, I felt led to read Hebrews 10. This chapter of the Bible is all about faith. In faith, I had applied for the job. In faith, I had proactively reduced my personal responsibilities in the form of extracurricular activities and service to prepare for what was to come. In faith, I started doing repairs on my home to make it more comfortable. Little did I know at the time that because of my faith fueled efforts, once those were completed the job offer would be extended. What I initially had faith for had now come to pass. So I was at a decisions crossroad and I needed to make one quickly.

I fell asleep after speaking with various individuals to hear what they thought about the decision but I still didn't have peace. When I woke up in the middle of the night I felt led to read Hebrews 10 and I knew right then that I should take the job and let God work out the rest. Much like in Exodus 3 God had a message for me. This experience, while one of many, taught me that faith is like a muscle, the more you exercise it, the stronger it becomes. My faith required me to obey and looking back I'm so glad I did because I not only gained new experiences, I met new people, and my faith continued to grow.

Daily Devotion (Day 12)

Gratitude: Today, I'm grateful for...
Every day is a gift! Use this space to reflect on what you are thankful for.

Dreams: I had a dream...
Use this space to document what you recall from your dreams so that you can ask the Holy Spirit to show you what it means. You can also use this space to document your vision based on what you believe will happen today, this week, or in the future.

Mediate: Today, I'm meditating on...
Use this section to highlight scriptures that you would like to meditate on.

Daily Devotion
Use this space to document what God is showing you as you navigate this 40-day journey.

Thirteen

Day 13 - Upon This Mountain

" "And he said, Certainly I will be with thee; and this shall " be a token unto thee, that I have sent thee: When thou hast brought forth the people out of Egypt, ye shall serve God upon this mountain." Exodus 3:12 KJV

Upon This Mountain

A mountain by definition is a mass of land and rock that rises at least 1,000 feet or more around the surrounding land and is sometimes formed through volcanic activity, or erosion. They can be seen as a single peak or sometimes part of a larger cluster which appear in a chain. When I researched the frequency of the word mountain in the bible I found sources that note the word was used over 300 times. Other estimates are as high as 500+ depending on the version of the bible you are reading. So why does this matter?

When we think about Exodus 3:12 Moses is advised that he will serve God upon this mountain also known as an elevation after he rescues the people out of Egypt. This reminds me of the fact that life is full of valleys and peaks, highs and lows. Akin to the friction that often creates the beautiful mountains we see, something occurred beneath the surface to cause the land mass to rise. I'd like to say, it's the story that we don't know since the shift is often out of sight.

Upon researching the Hebrew definition of the word mountain I found that in ancient times people believed that mountains symbolized being in the presence of God because of its proximity to the sky which makes a lot of sense. Mountains may evoke many emotions for individuals depending on their life experiences. Some may look upon a mountain with awe, while others may look at the mountain with angst due to the sheer size in comparison to people. Then there are the climbers, those who enjoy the challenge of getting to the top. All these things being considered there are times where we become stagnant, circling the same mountain yet not being willing to take on the incline or move along. For instance, in Deuteronomy 2:3 the scripture notes "Ye have compassed this mountain long enough: turn you northward."

Today, consider where you are currently, as well as, the shifts you've encountered both highs and lows. Then ask God to bring to your remembrance the moments and memories that have brought you closer to God.

Daily Devotion (Day 13)

Gratitude: Today, I'm grateful for...

Every day is a gift! Use this space to reflect on what you are thankful for.

Dreams: I had a dream...

Use this space to document what you recall from your dreams so that you can ask the Holy Spirit to show you what it means. You can also use this space to document your vision based on what you believe will happen today, this week, or in the future.

Mediate: Today, I'm meditating on...
Use this section to highlight scriptures that you would like to meditate on.

Daily Devotion
Use this space to document what God is showing you as you navigate this 40-day journey.

Fourteen

Day 14 - Listen Up

❝   "And Moses said unto the Lord, O my Lord, I am not ❞
eloquent, neither heretofore, nor since thou hast spoken
unto thy servant: but I am slow of speech, and of a slow
tongue. And the Lord said unto him, Who hath made man's
mouth? or who maketh the dumb, or deaf, or the seeing,
or the blind? have not I the Lord? Now therefore go, and I
will be with thy mouth, and teach thee what thou shalt say."
Exodus 4:10-12 KJV

Listen Up

In Exodus 4 God gave Moses instructions yet he continued to question God's call because he didn't believe God could use him. Moses gave God every excuse he could think of in the moment to avoid the call on his life. If we are honest, how many of us have done the same thing. Wondering how can God use someone like me? So let's look at Moses' excuses.

Excuse 1

"And Moses answered and said, But, behold, they will not believe me, nor hearken unto my voice: for they will say, The Lord hath not appeared unto thee." Exodus 4:1 KJV

There are several instances in the bible where the people God called were afraid to answer because they feared the faces of men (other people). How often in life do we fear the opinions of people and make excuses for why we don't do what God has put in our heart to do. At the end of our lives we have to give an account for how we spent our time, how we used our treasure, and how we multiplied our talent. One lesson I can honestly say I've learned the hard way is valuing the opinions of others over my spiritual convictions and calling. This is partly why many of my personal goals were delayed. My hope is that God will redeem the time and give me ample opportunity to fulfill what I feel in my heart is my calling. We all have a role in the kingdom of God which is to further the gospel of Jesus Christ yet how we do it may vary depending on the gifts and talents God has given us. Read Matthew 25 and Luke 19 to get a clearer understanding of the parables in which talents are discussed.

Excuse 2

"And Moses said unto the Lord, O my Lord, I am not eloquent, neither heretofore, nor since thou hast spoken unto thy servant: but I am slow of speech, and of a slow tongue. And the Lord said unto him, Who hath made man's mouth? or who maketh the dumb, or deaf, or the seeing, or the blind? have not I the Lord? Now therefore go, and I will be with thy mouth, and teach thee what thou shalt say." Exodus 4:10-12 KJV

Excuses, excuses. The Word reminds us that we are fearfully and wonderfully made in Psalm 139:14 yet like Moses, we may sometimes question why God made us a certain way. The world would have us believing we are not enough because we don't fit the societal mold yet God's kingdom is not like society. When I read Exodus 4 I started to understand why Godly confidence is necessary because it's rooted in faith not pride. Pride focuses on what we can do, faith focuses on what God can produce.

Today, think about the excuses that are holding you back and write them down so that you can see what may be hindering your personal growth with God. From there, find scriptures to counteract those negative thoughts. If we fill our minds with positivity, it will flow to and through our hearts versus the alternative. After all Luke 6:45 reminds us "for of the abundance of the heart his mouth speaketh."

Daily Devotion (Day 14)

Gratitude: Today, I'm grateful for...
Every day is a gift! Use this space to reflect on what you are thankful for.

Dreams: I had a dream...
Use this space to document what you recall from your dreams so that you can ask the Holy Spirit to show you what it means. You can also use this space to document your vision based on what you believe will happen today, this week, or in the future.

Mediate: Today, I'm meditating on...
Use this section to highlight scriptures that you would like to meditate on.

Daily Devotion
Use this space to document what God is showing you as you navigate this 40-day journey.

Fifteen

Day 15 - Plagued

"And the Lord said unto Moses, Rise up early in the morning, and stand before Pharaoh, and say unto him, Thus saith the Lord God of the Hebrews, Let my people go, that they may serve me. For I will at this time send all my plagues upon thine heart, and upon thy servants, and upon thy people; that thou mayest know that there is none like me in all the earth. For now I will stretch out my hand, that I may smite thee and thy people with pestilence; and thou shalt be cut off from the earth. And in very deed for this cause have I raised thee up, for to shew in thee my power; and that my name may be declared throughout all the earth." Exodus 9:13-16 KJV

Plagued

Have you seen the news today? I think it's time to watch and pray. Luke 21 reminds us about the signs of the end times but there is also a promise of hope that if we watch and pray we may be able to escape these things. When I think about what's happening today and Exodus 9 I see many parallels to prophetic words in the bible and those who have been sent forth for such a time as this. God told Moses to rise early and advise Pharaoh of what was to come if he didn't listen to God's command and let his people go. As we know, Moses had to repeatedly ask Pharaoh to let God's people go and his hardened heart stopped him from giving in. As a result, the Egyptian people suffered the consequences.

When we look at some leaders today, their hearts are hardened against the children of God. Yet we see the captives being set free albeit differently. For instance, those who have committed crimes against others are no longer being able to hide behind their shields because their unrepentant hearts have been turned over to God's judgment. Rather than repent to God and apologize for faults, some would rather risk their life for the lie. What I mean by this is, they would rather live a lie than confess their wrongdoings, repent, and turn from their wicked and deceitful ways. I cannot say that God's conviction or correction feels good yet it's necessary. Speaking from personal experience I understand now why the bible says the truth will set us free (John 8:32). It recently dawned on me that God cannot heal what we choose not to reveal. It's not that God doesn't know, it's that he loves us enough to give us a choice to choose Him.

As you reflect on your life, where you are, and where you've been, consider the areas in which you feel like your heart is hardened and ask

God to show you what it takes to remove the stony heart and replace it with a heart of flesh (Ezekiel 36).

Daily Devotion (Day 15)

Gratitude: Today, I'm grateful for...
Every day is a gift! Use this space to reflect on what you are thankful for.

Dreams: I had a dream...
Use this space to document what you recall from your dreams so that you can ask the Holy Spirit to show you what it means. You can also use this space to document your vision based on what you believe will happen today, this week, or in the future.

Mediate: Today, I'm meditating on...
Use this section to highlight scriptures that you would like to meditate on.

Daily Devotion
Use this space to document what God is showing you as you navigate this 40-day journey.

Sixteen

Day 16 - Covenant Keeper

"And I will take you to me for a people, and I will be to you a God: and ye shall know that I am the Lord your God, which bringeth you out from under the burdens of the Egyptians. And I will bring you in unto the land, concerning the which I did swear to give it to Abraham, to Isaac, and to Jacob; and I will give it you for an heritage: I am the Lord." Exodus 6:7-8 KJV

Covenant Keeper

There was a time in my life where I viewed my relationship with God through the lens of my experiences with people. All I can say is, whew, what a difficult time! I say it was difficult because people will let you down which ultimately impacts your heart posture. In fact, Proverbs 13:12 reminds us that "Hope deferred maketh the heart sick: but when the desire cometh, it is a tree of life." So, what is hope?

Hope by definition means a feeling of expectation that something will happen. It is a feeling that we can trust what we believe will come to pass. As a result when we don't get what we "hope for" it can make our "heart sick." Sickness in Hebrew refers to the state of being ill, grieved, or afflicted. Some of us have been afflicted by people or situations that we encounter in life. Repeated exposure to these experiences can sometimes rob our heart of gladness which literally and figuratively makes us sick. In fact, Proverbs 4:23 indicates "Keep thy heart with all diligence; for out of it are the issues of life." These issues sometimes make us less hopeful and therefore less dependent on God. When people let us down we stop expecting them to come through but when we apply this same logic to God, we miss out on the blessing and opportunity by trusting that God's Word is true.

Today, I encourage you to truly reflect on the current state of your heart and ask yourself honestly, is my heart sick? Seriously, you deserve to be happy so give this some thought. What I've found is in times of extreme pain and grief we feel all the feels yet when things level out and subside we can still be slowly dying inside because our hope is gone. Once you take stock of where you are, repent for hardening your heart, renounce any prior covenants with brokenness, and replace those negative thoughts with the Word of God. In fact, find 2-3 scriptures to counteract any negative feelings you feel, e.g., abandonment, rejection, etc. This exercise may bring up some unexpected feelings but on the other side of that pain I promise there is so much more to gain. When God brings you out, you don't have to doubt! Why? He is a covenant keeper.

Daily Devotion (Day 16)

Gratitude: Today, I'm grateful for...
Every day is a gift! Use this space to reflect on what you are thankful for.

Dreams: I had a dream...
Use this space to document what you recall from your dreams so that you can ask the Holy Spirit to show you what it means. You can also use this space to document your vision based on what you believe will happen today, this week, or in the future.

Mediate: Today, I'm meditating on...

Use this section to highlight scriptures that you would like to meditate on.

Daily Devotion

Use this space to document what God is showing you as you navigate this 40-day journey.

Seventeen

Day 17 - Passover

" "Then Moses called for all the elders of Israel, and said " unto them, Draw out and take you a lamb according to your families, and kill the passover. And ye shall take a bunch of hyssop, and dip it in the blood that is in the bason, and strike the lintel and the two side posts with the blood that is in the bason; and none of you shall go out at the door of his house until the morning. For the Lord will pass through to smite the Egyptians; and when he seeth the blood upon the lintel, and on the two side posts, the Lord will pass over the door, and will not suffer the destroyer to come in unto your houses to smite you. And ye shall observe this thing for an ordinance to thee and to thy sons for ever." Exodus 12:21-24 KJV

Passover

Passover also known as Pesach was a time of sacrifice and mercy. In Exodus 12 the children of God were given explicit instructions that they had to obey in order for their homes to be spared when the destroyer passed over Egypt.

"For I will pass through the land of Egypt this night, and will smite all the firstborn in the land of Egypt, both man and beast; and against all the gods of Egypt I will execute judgment: I am the Lord. And the blood shall be to you for a token upon the houses where ye are: and when I see the blood, I will pass over you, and the plague shall not be upon you to destroy you, when I smite the land of Egypt." Exodus 12:12-13 KJV

When the destroyer came in Exodus 12:29-30 there was a cry throughout Egypt because "there was not a house where there was not one dead." Yet, those who obeyed God, His children, were spared. "And it came to pass the selfsame day, that the Lord did bring the children of Israel out of the land of Egypt by their armies." Exodus 12:51 KJV

When we think about God's covenant, and his Word, we know that God will do what He says He will do and that also includes concerning you. One thing to note however are the conditions. Sometimes we expect God to come through but we don't do what we need to. Exodus 12 is a great illustration of this. God required his children to obey before the promise could come to pass. Because they obeyed they were able to receive the blessing God had before them. As you reflect on Exodus 12 consider the areas in which God is calling you to obey. What does God have to say?

Daily Devotion (Day 17)

Gratitude: Today, I'm grateful for...
Every day is a gift! Use this space to reflect on what you are thankful for.

Dreams: I had a dream...
Use this space to document what you recall from your dreams so that you can ask the Holy Spirit to show you what it means. You can also use this space to document your vision based on what you believe will happen today, this week, or in the future.

Mediate: Today, I'm meditating on...

Use this section to highlight scriptures that you would like to meditate on.

Daily Devotion

Use this space to document what God is showing you as you navigate this 40-day journey.

Eighteen

Day 18 - Remember the Times

"The Lord your God which goeth before you, he shall fight for you, according to all that he did for you in Egypt before your eyes; And in the wilderness, where thou hast seen how that the Lord thy God bare thee, as a man doth bear his son, in all the way that ye went, until ye came into this place. Yet in this thing ye did not believe the Lord your God, Who went in the way before you, to search you out a place to pitch your tents in, in fire by night, to shew you by what way ye should go, and in a cloud by day." Deuteronomy 1:30-33 KJV

Remember the Times

Often times when we make it out of the madness of life we sometimes forget God. In Deuteronomy 1 the children of God are reminded about the fact that they were brought out of captivity by the Lord their God yet after they crossed over the Red Sea, they reverted back to woe is me. This is actually quite common and akin to hedonic adaptation where an individual's relative state of happiness returns to its baseline after a period of time. This is often during the period in which things go back to normal. For example, imagine the feeling of buying a new car or house. We are often excited at the onset but after that new car or house starts to settle we begin to settle too. As a result, what made us happy yesterday no longer suffices for today.

It is important to take note of this because it's easy to go astray when we are not mindful nor appreciative of the blessings we have. Gratitude is a great remedy for murmuring and complaining because it helps us put things in perspective so that we don't squander the blessing looking for the next big thing. In fact, murmuring and complaining is what kept the children of God from inheriting God's promised land. Deuteronomy 1:34-35 reads "And the Lord heard the voice of your words, and was wroth, and sware, saying, Surely there shall not one of these men of this evil generation see that good land, which I sware to give unto your fathers."

Today, reflect on what you are grateful for that you may have forgotten about and make a list. This will help you inventory where you are and ideally where you want to be in terms of God's economy.

Daily Devotion (Day 18)

Gratitude: Today, I'm grateful for...
Every day is a gift! Use this space to reflect on what you are thankful for.

Dreams: I had a dream...
Use this space to document what you recall from your dreams so that you can ask the Holy Spirit to show you what it means. You can also use this space to document your vision based on what you believe will happen today, this week, or in the future.

Mediate: Today, I'm meditating on...

Use this section to highlight scriptures that you would like to meditate on.

Daily Devotion

Use this space to document what God is showing you as you navigate this 40-day journey.

Nineteen

Day 19 - Follow the Instructions

"Then ye answered and said unto me, We have sinned against the Lord, we will go up and fight, according to all that the Lord our God commanded us. And when ye had girded on every man his weapons of war, ye were ready to go up into the hill. And the Lord said unto me, Say unto them. Go not up, neither fight; for I am not among you; lest ye be smitten before your enemies. So I spake unto you; and ye would not hear, but rebelled against the commandment of the Lord, and went presumptuously up into the hill. And the Amorites, which dwelt in that mountain, came out against you, and chased you, as bees do, and destroyed you in Seir, even unto Hormah. And ye returned and wept before the Lord; but the Lord would not hearken to your voice, nor give ear unto you." Deuteronomy 1:41-45 KJV

Follow the Instructions

One thing about God, He doesn't play about His instructions. This doesn't mean that God doesn't have compassion, but He reminds us in Romans 9 that his mercy is shown to those whom he chooses.

"What shall we say then? Is there unrighteousness with God? God forbid. For he saith to Moses, I will have mercy on whom I will have mercy, and I will have compassion on whom I will have compassion. So then it is not of him that willeth, nor of him that runneth, but of God that sheweth mercy. For the scripture saith unto Pharaoh, Even for this same purpose have I raised thee up, that I might shew my power in thee, and that my name might be declared throughout all the earth. Therefore hath he mercy on whom he will have mercy, and whom he will he hardeneth." Romans 9:14-18 KJV

When I read this initially I was somewhat taken aback because I didn't have a clear understanding. Yet, when I allowed the Holy Spirit to minister to my heart things started to become more clear. When we murmur and complain like the Israelites, we lose out on the power that comes from humbling ourselves before God and remembering who He is in our lives as well as what He has done. When we have the spirit of God with us we can achieve great things yet when we sin against the Lord we separate ourselves from His power, grace, and mercy. For instance in Deuteronomy 1, the Israelites were instructed not to fight because they would lose. Yet because of pride and disobedience the Word says they went presumptuously up into the hill and were chased away. It was at this point they realized what they had done yet the Lord would not hear their voices because of the sin that separated them and the spirit of rebellion that caused them to err even after being warned.

God corrects those whom he loves and we know that He loves us through faith yet it's still a choice to heed the correction (Hebrews 12). In the case of the Israelites, they murmured and complained and then chose to disregard God's warning. In doing so, they ended up on a different path. Did God still take care of them? He did; however, it was after they repented. That being said, there were consequences for their disobedience. I like to think of the consequences as detours. God may give us the map but it's up to us to make the right turns. When we decide to deviate from the plan it may require a detour because the best path is not available anymore. Take for instance when God gives us an idea and we fail to act during the timeframe in which God asked us to do something. According to 1 Samuel 15:23 "For rebellion is as the sin of witchcraft, and stubbornness is as iniquity and idolatry." In fact, the scripture goes on to say "Because thou hast rejected the word of the Lord, he hath also rejected thee from being king." When we know what we ought to do and we fail to do it, it's only God's grace and mercy that can grant us another chance. In Saul's case, his failure to obey cost him his role as King. This is one of many examples in the Bible where we see God's mercy shift according to His children's willingness to obey.

Ask God to show you any areas in your life where you have been disobedient and jot them down. Next, repent for your rebellion, renounce coming into agreement with the enemy to delay God's call, and replace any covenants with the enemy in the form of laziness, procrastination, etc. with the Word of God. My hope is that God will show us mercy yet we have a requirement too, to listen to the voice of the Holy Spirit and accept whatever God tells us to do.

Gratitude: Today, I'm grateful for...
Every day is a gift! Use this space to reflect on what you are thankful for.

Dreams: I had a dream...
Use this space to document what you recall from your dreams so that you can ask the Holy Spirit to show you what it means. You can also use this space to document your vision based on what you believe will happen today, this week, or in the future.

Mediate: Today, I'm meditating on...
Use this section to highlight scriptures that you would like to meditate on.

Daily Devotion
Use this space to document what God is showing you as you navigate this 40-day journey.

Twenty

Day 20 - Set Apart for Salvation

"The Lord is my strength and song, and he is become my salvation: he is my God, and I will prepare him an habitation; my father's God, and I will exalt him." Exodus 15:2 KJV

Set Apart for Salvation

Salvation means to set apart from harm or ruin. When we think about the example of the Israelites journey to freedom and the plagues that God sent after warning Pharaoh to "let my people go," it is even more evident that God's children were set apart and shown mercy and favor. The grace upon their lives is what troubled Pharaoh because he was afraid that they would become mightier than the Egyptians yet God prevailed in setting the captives free.

The children of Israel were considered chosen as a result of God's covenant with their forefathers. God is not like people so He doesn't lie and His Word will never return to Him void. In true fashion, He upheld His part of the agreement.

Fast forward to the New Testament and salvation to the believer is referring to being granted the eternal gift of life through the power of Jesus Christ. It sets us free from damnation and condemnation yet there is something we must do. Acts 16 is a powerful illustration of this. Paul and Silas freed a woman from the spirit of divination (fortune-telling) and were jailed because her "Masters" were angry that "the hope of their gains were gone." As a result they brought Paul and Silas to the magistrates and in verses 20-21 said "These men, being Jews, do exceedingly trouble our city, And teach customs, which are not lawful for us to receive, neither to observe, being Romans." Paul and Silas were then beat and jailed. At midnight Paul and Silas prayed and praised God and all of the prisoners heard them and suddenly there was a great earthquake which loosed their chains. Hallelujah! They were free yet they didn't leave. The keeper of the prison was distraught and thought he should take his own life because he was under the impression all of the prisoners escaped yet Paul and Silas cried out "Do thyself no harm: for we are all here." When he heard this he came to Paul and Silas trembling and asked "what must I do to be saved?" Paul and Silas said "Believe on the Lord Jesus Christ, and thou shalt be saved, and thy house" and so they were.

"And when it was day, the magistrates sent the serjeants, saying, Let those men go. And the keeper of the prison told this saying to Paul, The magistrates have sent to let you go: now therefore depart, and go in peace. But Paul said unto them, They have beaten us openly uncondemned, being Romans, and have cast us into prison; and now do they thrust us out privily? nay verily; but let them come themselves and fetch us out. And the serjeants told these words unto the magistrates: and they feared, when they heard that they were Romans. And they came and besought them, and brought them out, and desired them to depart out of the city." Acts 16:35-39 KJV

I love this story because there are so many parallels to life. The enemy attempts to bind us when we walk in God's grace, mercy, and freedom. Ideally he tries to hold us captive. When we "believe on the Lord Jesus Christ," pray, and praise God, the foundation of the enemy's lies become weaker and break. We are finally set free to be the men and women God called us to be. Today, read Acts 16, reflect on the many lessons, and thank God for the gift of salvation.

Gratitude: Today, I'm grateful for...

Every day is a gift! Use this space to reflect on what you are thankful for.

Dreams: I had a dream...

Use this space to document what you recall from your dreams so that you can ask the Holy Spirit to show you what it means. You can also use this space to document your vision based on what you believe will happen today, this week, or in the future.

Mediate: Today, I'm meditating on...

Use this section to highlight scriptures that you would like to meditate on.

Daily Devotion

Use this space to document what God is showing you as you navigate this 40-day journey.

Twenty-One

Day 21 - He Split the Red Sea for Me

> "And she said unto the men, I know that the Lord hath given you the land, and that your terror is fallen upon us, and that all the inhabitants of the land faint because of you. For we have heard how the Lord dried up the water of the Red sea for you, when ye came out of Egypt; and what ye did unto the two kings of the Amorites, that were on the other side Jordan, Sihon and Og, whom ye utterly destroyed. And as soon as we had heard these things, our hearts did melt, neither did there remain any more courage in any man, because of you: for the Lord your God, he is God in heaven above, and in earth beneath." Joshua 2:9-11 KJV

He Split the Red Sea for Me

Joshua 2 recounts the testimony of Rahab. If you know this story than you know that Rahab was known as a harlot (prostitute) yet she was granted mercy and favor when the Israelites returned to destroy the land because she hid the spies Joshua sent out. Before she did this, she spoke to the men (spies) acknowledging the fact that the Lord had given the people of Israel the land. She also shared how she knows God dried up the Red sea for them and that on the other side of Jordan they destroyed their enemies. Knowing this, the inhabitants of the land feared the Israelites because they knew that the Lord of the Israelites was God in heaven above and in the earth beneath.

Rahab then asked the spies to have mercy on her and her family when God gives them the land. The spies agreed as long as Rahab agreed to uphold her part of the bargain which was to spare their lives and in turn they would deal kindly with her when they returned. So the spies returned to Joshua with a better report and said in verse 24 "... Truly the Lord hath delivered into our hands all the land; for even all the inhabitants of the country do faint because of us."

There are so many lessons that we can glean from this chapter but I'd like to focus on two in particular because they are powerful. The first being, God can use whom he chooses. Rahab was a harlot yet she feared the Lord. Hebrews 11:31 reads "By faith the harlot Rahab perished not with them that believed not, when she had received the spies with peace." Second, it's to be obedient. Rahab told the spies in verse 16 "...Get you to the mountain, lest the pursuers meet you; and hide yourselves there three days, until the pursuers be returned: and afterward may ye go your way." Had the spies not received the warning they may have been captured thereby further delaying the Israelites entering into the promised land.

When we think about our own lives, it's important to consider where we are being hindered due to a lack of faith. Similarly, it will be important for us to examine our hearts regarding where we've been obedient as well as the areas that we know we've been disobedient so we can ask God for forgiveness and another opportunity to get it right so the wilderness won't be our plight.

Daily Devotion (Day 21)

Gratitude: Today, I'm grateful for...

Every day is a gift! Use this space to reflect on what you are thankful for.

Dreams: I had a dream...

Use this space to document what you recall from your dreams so that you can ask the Holy Spirit to show you what it means. You can also use this space to document your vision based on what you believe will happen today, this week, or in the future.

Mediate: Today, I'm meditating on...
Use this section to highlight scriptures that you would like to meditate on.

Daily Devotion
Use this space to document what God is showing you as you navigate this 40-day journey.

Twenty-Two

Day 22 - God Made a Way

"When thou passest through the waters, I will be with thee; and through the rivers, they shall not overflow thee: when thou walkest through the fire, thou shalt not be burned; neither shall the flame kindle upon thee." Isaiah 43:2 KJV

God Made a Way

One thing I've been reminded of since I started writing this devotional is that God will always make a way when we do things His way. It's so tempting to try and get ahead of God but I've learned He knows best because His timing is often what we need to learn and grow. Sometimes I've tried to rush a process because I just want it to be done while God may want me to learn a lesson in the valley so when I reach the mountain peak there won't be something that I've failed to deal with seeking to hinder me.

Habakkuk 2:3 reminds us "For the vision is yet for an appointed time, but at the end it shall speak, and not lie: though it tarry, wait for it; because it will surely come, it will not tarry." In Hebrew the word tarry means "to remain behind." Feeling like you should be further along can sometimes subtract from your internal motivation bank. That being said, God always knows what is to come and often gives us time and opportunity to prepare.

Speaking of preparation, I have several examples of this especially as it relates to job opportunities. In one instance, I recall not being selected for 10+ training jobs with a former employer. I started to become discouraged because I believed training and development was my career calling yet God was showing me that the timing wasn't right. Since I wasn't sure when I would hear "yes" I decided that I would continue to do my best. I also noticed that with each interview I gained valuable insights into what I could expect and I also started to develop a tougher mental attitude as an added bonus. While there were many denials, hearing "yes" was always welcome.

Today, consider where you are, and where you want to be, so you can confidently say, "God won't delay what is in store for me".

Daily Devotion (Day 22)

Gratitude: Today, I'm grateful for...
Every day is a gift! Use this space to reflect on what you are thankful for.

Dreams: I had a dream...
Use this space to document what you recall from your dreams so that you can ask the Holy Spirit to show you what it means. You can also use this space to document your vision based on what you believe will happen today, this week, or in the future.

Mediate: Today, I'm meditating on...
Use this section to highlight scriptures that you would like to meditate on.

Daily Devotion
Use this space to document what God is showing you as you navigate this 40-day journey.

Twenty-Three

Day 23 - God's Gift

" "Turn again, and tell Hezekiah the captain of my people, "
Thus saith the Lord, the God of David thy father, I have heard
thy prayer, I have seen thy tears: behold, I will heal thee: on
the third day thou shalt go up unto the house of the Lord.
And I will add unto thy days fifteen years; and I will deliver
thee and this city out of the hand of the king of Assyria; and
I will defend this city for mine own sake, and for my servant
David's sake." 2 Kings 20:5-6 KJV

God's Gift

God reminded me that time is a gift yet often times we squander it focused on things that we think matter because they are visible or tangible. When we read Hezekiah's testimony in 2 Kings 20:1 it notes "In those days was Hezekiah sick unto death. And the prophet Isaiah the son of Amoz came to him, and said unto him, Thus saith the Lord, Set thine house in order; for thou shalt die, and not live."

In the verses that followed Hezekiah humbled himself and prayed unto the Lord to ask for more time. God heard his cry and granted his petition of healing, in addition to giving him 15 more years of life. When I think about God's gifts, what comes to mind is salvation, mercy, and grace. Speaking from personal experience, I know that there are times where I have taken God's grace for granted. I no longer want to live that way yet I recognize that there are so many distractions designed to lead us astray. The enemy of our soul, Satan, rejoices because we are easily deceived by a lot of the things that we see. Luke 21 reminds us that this will only get worse in the end times.

While writing this book I became distracted and I was immediately convicted by the Holy Spirit. The Holy Spirit showed me that I have sometimes put people in first place, social media, work, and the like yet I am grateful for the conviction because Hebrews 12:5 reminds us "For whom the Lord loveth he chasteneth, and scourgeth [afflicts] every son whom he receiveth." While on the surface, this doesn't seem like something that would bring excitement, I have come to learn that godly correction is necessary to live a full and fruitful life.

Today, consider the ways in which God has shown you mercy through Holy Spirit conviction.

Daily Devotion (Day 23)

Gratitude: Today, I'm grateful for...
Every day is a gift! Use this space to reflect on what you are thankful for.

Dreams: I had a dream...
Use this space to document what you recall from your dreams so that you can ask the Holy Spirit to show you what it means. You can also use this space to document your vision based on what you believe will happen today, this week, or in the future.

Mediate: Today, I'm meditating on...
Use this section to highlight scriptures that you would like to meditate on.

Daily Devotion
Use this space to document what God is showing you as you navigate this 40-day journey.

Twenty-Four

Day 24 - No Complaints

> "And the Lord said unto me, Say unto them. Go not up, neither fight; for I am not among you; lest ye be smitten before your enemies." Deuteronomy 1:42 KJV

No Complaints

In Deuteronomy 1, the children of Israel had been wandering around the same mountain in the wilderness for 40 years. As I reflect on my 40 years of life, I don't think it's strange that God put this vision in my heart. God told me to possess the land (his promises) yet I let fear of giants (people, failure, mockery, etc.,) slow me down. It's so easy to erect idols (anything we put before God) in our hearts and minds because in most cases they lie dormant.

I'm grateful that our God is merciful and his love towards us endures. One of the primary things I've learned is that we must remain humble and acknowledge when we stumble. My hope is that I won't be denied like Moses and the children of Israel, who mumbled and complained in their wilderness. If this resonates with you, my desire is that you too will get another opportunity for breakthrough. May we have another chance to possess the promised land. Yet even if we don't, we can be grateful that our eyes have been opened and thank God for the relationship that has been strengthened along the journey. The outcome may not be the same, yet it is God that doesn't change.

"Then I said unto you, Dread not, neither be afraid of them [the giants]. The Lord your God which goeth before you, he shall fight for you, according to all that he did for you in Egypt before your eyes; And in the wilderness, where thou hast seen how that the Lord thy God bare thee, as a man doth bear his son, in all the way that ye went, until ye came into this place. Yet in this thing ye did not believe the Lord your God," Deuteronomy 1:29-32 KJV

Deuteronomy cut me to the core because what I can clearly see is that our walk requires faith at all times not just when things look or feel easy. So I'm learning to depend on God wholeheartedly and I hope that you will be able to do so too.

Daily Devotion (Day 24)

Gratitude: Today, I'm grateful for...
Every day is a gift! Use this space to reflect on what you are thankful for.

Dreams: I had a dream...
Use this space to document what you recall from your dreams so that you can ask the Holy Spirit to show you what it means. You can also use this space to document your vision based on what you believe will happen today, this week, or in the future.

Mediate: Today, I'm meditating on...
Use this section to highlight scriptures that you would like to meditate on.

Daily Devotion
Use this space to document what God is showing you as you navigate this 40-day journey.

Twenty-Five

Day 25 - Idol Lies

"" "Up, sanctify the people, and say, Sanctify yourselves "" against to morrow: for thus saith the Lord God of Israel, There is an accursed thing in the midst of thee, O Israel: thou canst not stand before thine enemies, until ye take away the accursed thing from among you." Joshua 7:13 KJV

Idol Lies

Whenever the children of Israel were given instructions to possess a land there were also specific directions given regarding what could be conquered, destroyed, and saved. Much like what we often witness today and/or perhaps have been a party to is willful disobedience regarding why God may have shared with us directly or indirectly what we are called to do before we get to where we are going. For instance in Joshua 7:11-12 the scripture reads:

> "Israel hath sinned, and they have also transgressed my covenant which I commanded them: for they have even taken of the accursed thing, and have also stolen, and dissembled also, and they have put it even among their own stuff. Therefore the children of Israel could not stand before their enemies, but turned their backs before their enemies, because they were accursed: neither will I be with you any more, except ye destroy the accursed from among you."

God was very serious about having an accursed item in the midst of his children because when they took possession of it, whatever it happened to be, God's grace would leave. In fact in the scripture above Joshua was told after losing the battle in Ai that the reason they lost was due to an item within their camp. Upon hearing why, Joshua rose early in the morning and "brought Israel by their tribes" to figure out who was responsible.

> "And Joshua said unto Achan, My son, give, I pray thee, glory to the Lord God of Israel, and make confession unto him; and tell me now what thou hast done; hide it not from me. And Achan answered Joshua, and said, Indeed I have sinned against the Lord God of Israel, and thus and thus have I done: When I saw among the spoils a goodly

Babylonish garment, and two hundred shekels of silver, and a wedge of gold of fifty shekels weight, then I coveted them, and took them; and, behold, they are hid in the earth in the midst of my tent, and the silver under it." Joshua 7:19-21 KJV

Much like Achan, we sometimes covet things that God is not concerned with because he has already given explicit instruction. Coveting in Hebrew refers to the act of desiring something or taking pleasure in it. Achan knew exactly what he was doing when he took the accursed items because much like Adam and Eve in the garden, he hid what he had done from others yet he couldn't hide it from God. Achan received the same instruction Joshua told the people in Joshua 6:18 "And ye, in any wise keep yourselves from the accursed thing, lest ye make yourselves accursed, when ye take of the accursed thing, and make the camp of Israel a curse, and trouble it." Achan's decisions troubled the camp and ultimately they all suffered the consequences until the accursed thing was removed. Achan, his family, and possessions including oxen, asses (donkeys), and sheep paid for his poor decisions with their lives much like the enemies they had previously destroyed. According to Joshua 7:26, until this day, a heap of stones lay in the valley of Achor.

While writing this chapter what came to mind is Proverbs 26:6, "Eat thou not the bread of him that hath an evil eye, neither desire thou his dainty meats:" because we can easily become distracted with the ways of the world falling back into sin again and again. Now, more than ever, it's imperative that we judge things righteously and not simply by appearances. We should also ask God for wisdom and discernment so when and/or if we fall, we can get back up again versus falling into mischief because we willfully choose to sin.

Daily Devotion (Day 25)

Gratitude: Today, I'm grateful for...

Every day is a gift! Use this space to reflect on what you are thankful for.

Dreams: I had a dream...

Use this space to document what you recall from your dreams so that you can ask the Holy Spirit to show you what it means. You can also use this space to document your vision based on what you believe will happen today, this week, or in the future.

Mediate: Today, I'm meditating on...
Use this section to highlight scriptures that you would like to meditate on.

Daily Devotion
Use this space to document what God is showing you as you navigate this 40-day journey.

Twenty-Six

Day 26 - Grace and Mercy

"Forty years old was I when Moses the servant of the Lord sent me from Kadeshbarnea to espy out the land; and I brought him word again as it was in mine heart. Nevertheless my brethren that went up with me made the heart of the people melt: but I wholly followed the Lord my God. And Moses sware on that day, saying, Surely the land whereon thy feet have trodden shall be thine inheritance, and thy children's for ever, because thou hast wholly followed the Lord my God. And now, behold, the Lord hath kept me alive, as he said, these forty and five years, even since the Lord spake this word unto Moses, while the children of Israel wandered in the wilderness: and now, lo, I am this day fourscore and five years old. As yet I am as strong this day as I was in the day that Moses sent me: as my strength was then, even so is my strength now, for war, both to go out, and to come in."
Joshua 14:7-11 KJV

Grace and Mercy

I've heard many people say "if God brings you to it, He will also bring you through it." While this may be true there is some work that we must do. We all have free will and therefore we have to choose to keep God's commandments and believe in who God says that He is.

In Joshua 14 we read how God preserved Joshua's strength for 45 years so that he could bring the next generation into the promised land. When we reflect on Numbers 13, Joshua and Caleb were the only two spies to bring a good report. All other spies were afraid and focused on the strength of the giants not their God. As the people murmured and complained Joshua and Caleb spoke up.

"At the same time, two of those who had explored the land, Joshua (son of Nun) and Caleb (son of Jephunneh), tore their clothes in despair. They said to the whole community of Israel, "The land we explored is very good. If the Lord is pleased with us, he will bring us into this land and give it to us. This is a land flowing with milk and honey! Don't rebel against the Lord, and don't be afraid of the people of the land. We will devour them like bread. They have no protection, and the Lord is with us. So don't be afraid of them." But when the whole community of Israel talked about stoning Moses and Aaron to death, they all saw the glory of the Lord shining at the tent of meeting. The Lord said to Moses, "How long will these people treat me with contempt? How long will they refuse to trust me in spite of all the miraculous signs I have done among them?" Numbers 14:6-11 KJV

Joshua and Caleb got it but the others let the fear of men fill their hearts with sin. In Numbers 14 God speaks of the necessity of trust especially given the "miraculous signs" that we often take for granted.

The fact that we woke up today and have breath in our lungs is enough to give God praise. Waking up, while it may seem simple, is truly a gift of grace (unmerited favor) and mercy (compassion). When we leave our homes and return, grace and mercy. When we undergo trials and tribulation yet we are alive to share the testimony, grace and mercy. By this point I'm sure you get the picture. God wants us to trust Him wholeheartedly because He ultimately chooses who he will show grace and mercy. Romans 9:14 reads "...God said to Moses, "I will be kind to anyone I want to. I will be merciful to anyone I want to." Therefore, God's choice does not depend on a person's desire or effort, but on God's mercy.

Today, reflect on the moments and memories in which you have been shown grace and mercy. Consider how you felt as well as the stage of life you were in. Reflection is a powerful tool to ensure we keep the right perspective and we don't forget where our help truly comes from.

Daily Devotion (Day 26)

Gratitude: Today, I'm grateful for...
Every day is a gift! Use this space to reflect on what you are thankful for.

Dreams: I had a dream...
Use this space to document what you recall from your dreams so that you can ask the Holy Spirit to show you what it means. You can also use this space to document your vision based on what you believe will happen today, this week, or in the future.

Mediate: Today, I'm meditating on...

Use this section to highlight scriptures that you would like to meditate on.

Daily Devotion

Use this space to document what God is showing you as you navigate this 40-day journey.

Twenty-Seven

Day 27 - Set Apart

" "But if ye will not drive out the inhabitants of the land from before you; then it shall come to pass, that those which ye let remain of them shall be pricks in your eyes, and thorns in your sides, and shall vex you in the land wherein ye dwell. Moreover it shall come to pass, that I shall do unto you, as I thought to do unto them." Numbers 33:55-56 KJV "

Set Apart

James 4:4 has a very direct warning for the believer "Ye adulterers and adulteresses, ye not that the friendship of the world is enmity with God? Whosoever therefore will be a friend of the world is the enemy of God." When I looked up the word enmity it means by definition to be actively opposed, hostile toward someone or something, or to have ill will. When we put the definition into context it makes a lot of sense. There are many believers who want to have it all because society tells us we can yet God strictly forbids certain behaviors.

Regarding sin, what I find interesting is that some people will weigh their behavior and the behavior of others on unbalanced scales. Meaning, we will sometimes minimize how we look at sin depending on which sin(s) we are engaged in. This is why nonbelievers sometimes label Christians as hypocritical since to God all sin is sin and will be judged. Growing up I really struggled with this because I often questioned how it could be possible that sin is the same, yet God brought to my remembrance Matthew 5 which reads:

"For I say unto you, That except your righteousness shall exceed the righteousness of the scribes and Pharisees, ye shall in no case enter into the kingdom of heaven. Ye have heard that it was said of them of old time, Thou shalt not kill; and whosoever shall kill shall be in danger of the judgment: But I say unto you, That whosoever is angry with his brother without a cause shall be in danger of the judgment: and whosoever shall say to his brother, Raca, shall be in danger of the council: but whosoever shall say, Thou fool, shall be in danger of hell fire." Matthew 5:20-22 KJV

The aforementioned scripture is from the chapter in which Jesus delivered his sermon on the mountain to the multitude that was gathered. It was during this same message that Jesus highlighted how and why we are set apart. In fact, Matthew 5:16 tells us to "Let your light so shine before men, that they may see your good works, and glorify your Father which is in heaven."

The command from Jesus was clear. Believers are set apart to bring God glory. To do so, we should be mindful of the life decisions we make, and the paths we decide to take, lest we end up before the judge (God) ill-prepared.

During the time in which this book was written I recall spilling something on my floor and I quickly bent down to clean it up. What came to mind as I was wiping up the spill was "when you make a mistake you clean/cover it up, yet when others make mistakes you comment." Boom, just like that I was convicted and corrected. I wasn't mad about it, in fact I was glad about it because it was a great illustration of what happens within the body of Christ. I was so glad God was dealing with me so He can heal me internally.

Have you had any personal encounters where God was showing you, you? If so, reflect on what it taught you. After all, according to Hebrews 12:6 God corrects us because He loves us.

Daily Devotion (Day 27)

Gratitude: Today, I'm grateful for...
Every day is a gift! Use this space to reflect on what you are thankful for.

Dreams: I had a dream...
Use this space to document what you recall from your dreams so that you can ask the Holy Spirit to show you what it means. You can also use this space to document your vision based on what you believe will happen today, this week, or in the future.

Mediate: Today, I'm meditating on...
Use this section to highlight scriptures that you would like to meditate on.

Daily Devotion
Use this space to document what God is showing you as you navigate this 40-day journey.

Twenty-Eight

Day 28 - Whose Report Will You Believe?

" Who hath believed our report? and to whom is the arm of the Lord revealed?" Isaiah 53:1 KJV

Whose Report Will You Believe?

My great aunt, Liz, was hospitalized September 23, 2023 after falling and breaking her femur. The reports from the doctors were grim, but God. They reported that her heart was weak which meant the required surgery was risky. When I arrived at the hospital upon hearing the news I remember feeling a lot of emotions. When I entered the room and overheard the doctor explaining to my grandmother my aunt's prognosis I left the room in tears because of what I was hearing. The doctor explained that she may have a few days to a few months to live and that she would never walk again. Our hearts were heavy because Aunt Liz has been a blessing to us all and to know she was literally fighting for her life was a feeling we knew all to well when God called her mother, my great-grandmother home. While we would miss her on this side, we know God is not a God that He should lie. So in those moments of uncertainty we could only hold on to our faith and hope that she would be okay for as long as the Lord would say that she could stay.

Upon returning home after visiting the hospital, I had many moments where I would cry, call out to God, and reminisce on the past. One of those days, I was sitting on my couch crying and I felt in my spirit, "at the end of the day, I have the last say!" It was in that moment a giant on the inside stood up and my faith was strengthened. From that point forward I would visit my aunt in the hospital, later in the nursing home, and eventually at home where we'd talk, pray, and praise God. Ironically during a few visits we had other family members and family friends who were also hospitalized. In fact, one day, while visiting Aunt Liz at the hospital I was notified that another great-aunt was in the same hospital due to heart issues so I had the opportunity to visit them both. When I visited my 2nd aunt, she stated in faith I am going home tomorrow. I cried, we prayed, and to God be the glory she is still here today. As I write this on July 24, 2024, my great aunt, Liz, is still alive by God's grace and celebrated her 84th birthday in May surrounded by family and friends. This is yet another testament to God's miracle working power which isn't the first time he has shown up and out in her life.

Two decades ago I received a phone call that Aunt Liz was sick and her kidneys weren't functioning which meant she would need to receive dialysis treatments. I remember the feelings as if it were yesterday because I recall knowing I needed to pray. Prayer brought peace, so when I went to the hospital I went with the expectation that at the end of the day God would have the last say. I hadn't heard it put that way at that point, but now as I reflect back I can now see that this was a truth I already knew. Upon arriving at the hospital from out of town, I went to her room. We chatted for a while before I decided to leave to buy her a coloring book and some crayons. Upon returning from the store, her doctor came in and said you can take her home. I was puzzled because I thought her kidney's weren't functioning. He then said something to the effect of "I don't know what happened but her kidney's are functioning again." In that moment all I could do was thank God. I helped her get dressed, and we left the hospital. This was certainly one of those God moments that I'll never forget because He was showing me back then that no matter what we face, there is absolutely nothing that can take God's place.

I started this daily devotion off with Isaiah 53 which is very fitting to me. Why? It chronicles the afflictions of Jesus as our Savior who knew no sin yet faced difficulties and trials over and over again.

> "He is despised and rejected of men; a man of sorrows, and acquainted with grief: and we hid as it were our faces from him; he was despised, and we esteemed him not. Surely he hath borne our griefs, and carried our sorrows: yet we did esteem him stricken, smitten of God, and afflicted. But he was wounded for our transgressions, he was

bruised for our iniquities: the chastisement of our peace was upon him; and with his stripes we are healed. All we like sheep have gone astray; we have turned every one to his own way; and the Lord hath laid on him the iniquity of us all." Isaiah 53:3-6 KJV

In spite of not deserving the afflictions he faced Jesus went through them anyway. As the Word reminds us, "by his stripes we are healed." I thank God for his grace and mercy and I hope this serves as an illustration for you too regarding just how much we need God no matter what we are going through.

Today, reflect on the times God has come through for you. How did you feel? What did you learn? Looking back, would you face your situation differently or do you believe everything happened just as it should be?

Daily Devotion (Day 28)

Gratitude: Today, I'm grateful for...
Every day is a gift! Use this space to reflect on what you are thankful for.

Dreams: I had a dream...
Use this space to document what you recall from your dreams so that you can ask the Holy Spirit to show you what it means. You can also use this space to document your vision based on what you believe will happen today, this week, or in the future.

Mediate: Today, I'm meditating on...

Use this section to highlight scriptures that you would like to meditate on.

Daily Devotion

Use this space to document what God is showing you as you navigate this 40-day journey.

Twenty-Nine

Day 29 - Anointed

> "The Spirit of the Lord is on me, because he has anointed me to preach the gospel to the poor; he hath sent me to heal the brokenhearted, to preach deliverance to the captives, and recovering sight to the blind, to set at liberty them that are bruised, To preach the acceptable year of the Lord."
> Luke 4:18-19 KJV

Anointed

In Luke 4 Jesus is tested in the wilderness for 40 days by the devil. He ate nothing during this time of testing yet he held on to the Words of God when the enemy tried to deceive him.

"Jesus, full of the Holy Spirit, left the Jordan and was led by the Spirit into the wilderness, where for forty days he was tempted by the devil. He ate nothing during those days, and at the end of them he was hungry. The devil said to him, "If you are the Son of God, tell this stone to become bread." Jesus answered, "It is written: 'Man shall not live on bread alone.' " The devil led him up to a high place and showed him in an instant all the kingdoms of the world. And he said to him, "I will give you all their authority and splendor; it has been given to me, and I can give it to anyone I want to. If you worship me, it will all be yours." Jesus answered, "It is written: 'Worship the Lord your God and serve him only.' " The devil led him to Jerusalem and had him stand on the highest point of the temple. "If you are the Son of God," he said, "throw yourself down from here. For it is written: " 'He will command his angels concerning you to guard you carefully; they will lift you up in their hands, so that you will not strike your foot against a stone.' " Jesus answered, "It is said: 'Do not put the Lord your God to the test.' " When the devil had finished all this tempting, he left him until an opportune time." Luke 4:1-13 KJV

When we think about life, this is exactly how the devil tricks us. He will give us a partial truth in hopes of us being deceived and following the path he sets out versus the path that God has for us. In the afore-mentioned scripture a few things stood out.

1. The enemy tempts us when we are in a vulnerable state. (Luke 4:1-2)
2. The enemy hopes we don't know the truth. (Luke 4:3-4)
3. The enemy presents false authority. (Luke 4:5-8)
4. The enemy knows the consequences of testing God. (Luke 4:9-12)
5. When we resist the enemy, he will flee. (Luke 4:13)

Same enemy, same strategy! When we observe what's happening today, we can see that the enemy still operates in the same way. He attempts to impart thoughts, feelings, and encourage people to engage in behaviors that he knows is detrimental to the person or those around them. For instance, Satan entered Judas so that he would betray Jesus since we know that his ultimate goal is to kill, steal, and destroy (Luke 22). Yet, when we are anointed, chosen, and protected by God, we can stand firm against the tricks of the enemy just like Jesus did. He was tempted yet he didn't fold in the face of the enemy nor any adversity. Instead, Jesus spoke boldly from a place of authority against the enemy. When we do this, we walk in the power of God to set others free from the enemy and the yokes that bind them (Luke 4:18-19).

May we continue to seek truth so we know how to handle temptation and can see the devil's tricks for what they are, false truths meant to deceive. Today, reflect on the times in which you've encountered the enemy's tricks in your life. What did they sound like? What scriptures can you add to your arsenal so you can proactively counteract any thoughts, beliefs, or behaviors that go against God's truth?

Daily Devotion (Day 29)

Gratitude: Today, I'm grateful for...
Every day is a gift! Use this space to reflect on what you are thankful for.

Dreams: I had a dream...
Use this space to document what you recall from your dreams so that you can ask the Holy Spirit to show you what it means. You can also use this space to document your vision based on what you believe will happen today, this week, or in the future.

Mediate: Today, I'm meditating on...
Use this section to highlight scriptures that you would like to meditate on.

Daily Devotion
Use this space to document what God is showing you as you navigate this 40-day journey.

Thirty

Day 30 - 10 Days Left

" "Cast not away therefore your confidence, which hath "
great recompence of reward. For ye have need of patience,
that, after ye have done the will of God, ye might receive
the promise. For yet a little while, and he that shall come
will come, and will not tarry. Now the just shall live by faith:
but if any man draw back, my soul shall have no pleasure in
him. But we are not of them who draw back unto perdition;
but of them that believe to the saving of the soul." Hebrews
10:35-39 KJV

10 Days Left

In September 2021 God spoke to my heart and told me to rename the CC: America Podcast to Confidence Restored. This was after a period of affliction in which I was angry, frustrated, and unclear regarding what was happening in my life. It was in this moment that God showed me confidence was not about how I felt about myself but it was more so about faith and trusting God in spite of what life situations look like.

I recall being at work on a Friday and nearing the close of business I stood up and was immediately coupled over in pain due to sciatic nerve issues. I realized walking was more difficult and called my mom to help with my daughter over the weekend because I knew there was no way I was going to be able to take care of her like I needed to if I couldn't even stand or sit without pain. I remember crying out in frustration because I could barely go up and down the stairs, sit comfortably, nor could I get in and out of bed. I remember expressing my frustration to my aunt Michelle who provided wise counsel considering where I was in life. I was an emotional wreck and needed to talk to God. While standing in the doorway of my bathroom crying and talking to God, I felt in my spirit, meaning a thought came to mind, which said, "you thought confidence was about you, but it's about me." I began to repent and praise God for the revelation and started speaking in faith that by the beginning of the following week I'd be well. Well, God is faithful and I haven't had sciatic nerve pain since. I believe I was healed by the power of Jesus Christ.

While I still struggled in other areas, God was showing me how deliverance worked, as well as, the necessity to trust Him in every season regardless of the reason. I now say, "when I don't know, and I can't see, I can trust that God is working some things out for me." So, "Cast not away therefore your confidence, which hath great recompence [payment] of reward. For ye have need of patience, that, after ye have done the will of God, ye might receive the promise." Hebrews 10:35-36 KJV

Today, reflect on the promises you are believing God for? What does it mean to wait patiently? Are you waiting well?

Daily Devotion (Day 30)

Gratitude: Today, I'm grateful for...
Every day is a gift! Use this space to reflect on what you are thankful for.

Dreams: I had a dream...
Use this space to document what you recall from your dreams so that you can ask the Holy Spirit to show you what it means. You can also use this space to document your vision based on what you believe will happen today, this week, or in the future.

Mediate: Today, I'm meditating on...
Use this section to highlight scriptures that you would like to meditate on.

Daily Devotion
Use this space to document what God is showing you as you navigate this 40-day journey.

Thirty-One

Day 31 - A New Covenant

"Behold, the days come, saith the Lord, that I will make a new covenant with the house of Israel, and with the house of Judah: Not according to the covenant that I made with their fathers in the day that I took them by the hand to bring them out of the land of Egypt; which my covenant they brake, although I was an husband unto them, saith the Lord: But this shall be the covenant that I will make with the house of Israel; After those days, saith the Lord, I will put my law in their inward parts, and write it in their hearts; and will be their God, and they shall be my people." Jeremiah 31:31-33 KJV

A New Covenant

God keeps His covenants, people break them!

This revelation came to me while writing this book because throughout the bible God speaks to and through others regarding the fact that God will honor his agreements as long as the conditions are met. We understand earthly covenants but we somehow struggle to understand why God has requirements for us too. Why? Could it be because we can't physically see God so we tend to put more faith in people. Or perhaps, it's a part of the enemy's deception on the earth.

Regardless of the why, one thing we can agree on is the fact that covenants, aka agreements, require us to adhere to certain conditions or standards of conduct. Think back to creation. The first covenant was between God and Adam.

"And the Lord God took the man, and put him into the garden of Eden to dress it and to keep it. And the Lord God commanded the man, saying, Of every tree of the garden thou mayest freely eat: But of the tree of the knowledge of good and evil, thou shalt not eat of it: for in the day that thou eatest thereof thou shalt surely die." Genesis 2:15-17 KJV

Well, we know how that story ends, welcome to the world of sin.

Other biblical covenants include Noah (Genesis 8-9), Abraham (Genesis 12-17), Moses (Exodus 19-24), and David (2 Samuel 7). God promises in Psalm 89:34-39 that his covenant He will not break while also highlighting the fallacy of men.

"My covenant will I not break, nor alter the thing that is gone out of my lips. Once have I sworn by my holiness that I will not lie unto David. His seed shall endure for ever, and his throne as the sun before me. It shall be established for ever as the moon, and as a faithful witness in heaven. Selah. But thou hast cast off and abhorred, thou hast been wroth with thine anointed. Thou hast made void the covenant of thy servant: thou hast profaned his crown by casting it to the ground."

To God be the glory we now have a new covenant through the sacrifice of Jesus Christ.

"Now the God of peace, that brought again from the dead our Lord Jesus, that great shepherd of the sheep, through the blood of the everlasting covenant, Make you perfect in every good work to do his will, working in you that which is wellpleasing in his sight, through Jesus Christ; to whom be glory for ever and ever. Amen." Hebrews 13:20-21 KJV

Much like covenants before, there is is something we must do. Romans 10:9 advises "that if you confess with your mouth the Lord Jesus and believe in your heart that God has raised Him from the dead, you will be saved." That being said, we can't sin our way into heaven after we repent. We must be willing to turn away from sin so that the grace of God can win. "For if we sin wilfully after that we have received the knowledge of the truth, there remaineth no more sacrifice for sins." Hebrews 10:26 KJV

Think about God's promises, as well as, the conditions. Are you currently passing the test? If not, repent to God and make a conscious decision to walk in righteousness with the power of the Holy Spirit.

"But he giveth more grace. Wherefore he saith, God resisteth the proud, but giveth grace unto the humble. Submit yourselves therefore to God. Resist the devil, and he will flee from you. Draw nigh to God, and he will draw nigh to you. Cleanse your hands, ye sinners; and purify your hearts, ye double minded. Be afflicted, and mourn, and weep: let your laughter be turned to mourning, and your joy to heaviness. Humble yourselves in the sight of the Lord, and he shall lift you up." James 4:6-10 KJV

Daily Devotion (Day 31)

Gratitude: Today, I'm grateful for...
Every day is a gift! Use this space to reflect on what you are thankful for.

Dreams: I had a dream...
Use this space to document what you recall from your dreams so that you can ask the Holy Spirit to show you what it means. You can also use this space to document your vision based on what you believe will happen today, this week, or in the future.

Mediate: Today, I'm meditating on...
Use this section to highlight scriptures that you would like to meditate on.

Daily Devotion
Use this space to document what God is showing you as you navigate this 40-day journey.

Thirty-Two

Day 32 - Rest

"Remember the word which Moses the servant of the Lord commanded you, saying, The Lord your God hath given you rest, and hath given you this land." Joshua 1:13 KJV

Rest

Rest is revolutionary!

When I looked up the definition of revolutionary, one definition means it can involve or be the catalyst for a major change. Other synonyms include words like innovative, out of the ordinary, and new. The opposing definition of revolutionary specifically speaks to politics and rebellion. In this case, I'm referring to the former; however, it's important to remember that the enemy corrupts what God gives us for a purpose. Satan's goals is to "kill, steal, and destroy" yet God wants to give us life per John 10:10.

Rest is a major part of this equation because when we do so purpose-fully it can improve our overall health. A lack of rest can also cost us which is why the enemy wants us to get so bogged down with the cares of life that we lose our faith and trust in God, our creator.

"But seek ye first the kingdom of God, and his righteousness; and all these things shall be added unto you. Take therefore no thought for the morrow: for the morrow shall take thought for the things of itself. Sufficient unto the day is the evil thereof." Matthew 6:33-34 KJV

Choosing to have faith and not worry ushers us into God's rest because we can trust that His words are true and will not fail. "So shall my word be that goeth forth out of my mouth: it shall not return unto me void, but it shall accomplish that which I please, and it shall prosper in the thing whereto I sent it." Isaiah 55:11 KJV

God's word is a catalyst for major change spiritually, mentally, and physically. In fact, Matthew 11:28 reads "Come unto me, all ye that labour and are heavy laden, and I will give you rest." Yet on the opposing side the Bible reminds us in Isaiah 48:22 that "There is no peace [rest], saith the Lord, unto the wicked." This message is repeated in Isaiah 57:21. So, why does this matter? It is a reminder that God created rest for a reason.

Rest rejuvenates the body, invigorates the mind, and replenishes the spirit. But like everything else the enemy tries to deceive us into corrupting the gift. God knows that physically we cannot function well when we don't get enough rest and the enemy knows it too because his goal is to get us out of God's will by staying on the proverbial hamster wheel.

So today, think about God's gift of rest. When He takes you to a new territory or land much like in Joshua 1:13, His intention is not for you to worry, it's to trust Him. When you reflect today, consider Hebrews 4:9-11 which reads:

"There remaineth therefore a rest to the people of God. For he that is entered into his rest, he also hath ceased from his own works, as God did from his. Let us labour therefore to enter into that rest, lest any man fall after the same example of unbelief."

Daily Devotion (Day 32)

Gratitude: Today, I'm grateful for...

Every day is a gift! Use this space to reflect on what you are thankful for.

Dreams: I had a dream...

Use this space to document what you recall from your dreams so that you can ask the Holy Spirit to show you what it means. You can also use this space to document your vision based on what you believe will happen today, this week, or in the future.

Mediate: Today, I'm meditating on...
Use this section to highlight scriptures that you would like to meditate on.

Daily Devotion
Use this space to document what God is showing you as you navigate this 40-day journey.

Thirty-Three

Day 33 - He Brought Me Here

"And I will sanctify my great name, which was profaned among the heathen, which ye have profaned in the midst of them; and the heathen shall know that I am the Lord, saith the Lord God, when I shall be sanctified in you before their eyes. For I will take you from among the heathen, and gather you out of all countries, and will bring you into your own land. Then will I sprinkle clean water upon you, and ye shall be clean: from all your filthiness, and from all your idols, will I cleanse you. A new heart also will I give you, and a new spirit will I put within you: and I will take away the stony heart out of your flesh, and I will give you an heart of flesh. And I will put my spirit within you, and cause you to walk in my statutes, and ye shall keep my judgments, and do them. And ye shall dwell in the land that I gave to your fathers; and ye shall be my people, and I will be your God."
Ezekiel 36:23-28 KJV

He Brought Me Here

Some things we face in life are a result of our personal choices. Other situations are by divine revelation and relationship. Ezekiel 36 reminds us of this, especially when we feel like we've arrived where we believe God wants us to be. Sometimes we are called to stand out where others want us to fit in. Sometimes we are called to speak truth to a heathen generation. Sometimes we go through the fire to show ourselves approved. And sometimes we shine bright because God wants us too. In every situation God is still God.

In today's society, it is easy to get caught up in the day-to-day minutia of it all and start looking like what we see versus who God has called us to be. In those instances, we are forsaking the gift of grace that God has bestowed upon us, and the mercy He has shown us.

When I think about arriving, being where you want to be, I think about the fact that some of us feel like we will be happy when instead of being grateful because. I have been guilty of thinking this way especially after starting something new. For example, getting a new job, cultivating a new relationship, or moving to a new location. Given my own personal experiences, I've learned that life changes and it's up to us to change with it or be left behind.

In Ezekiel 36, the scripture alludes to removing the stony heart and replacing it with a heart of flesh. I take this to mean being malleable, able to be molded and shaped by God's correction without losing heart. New opportunities are ripe with new challenges, but I'd venture to say you are much more equipped to deal with it, whatever "it" happens to be.

At the end of the day, God still cares and wants us to abide with the spirit of truth through any situation and in any place we find ourselves. I heard the Prophetess on The Master's Voice Prophecy Blog say recently, "God is looking for those who are looking for God." I wholeheartedly believe this to be true and my charge to you today is to reflect on how this applies to you.

Daily Devotion (Day 33)

Gratitude: Today, I'm grateful for...
Every day is a gift! Use this space to reflect on what you are thankful for.

Dreams: I had a dream...
Use this space to document what you recall from your dreams so that you can ask the Holy Spirit to show you what it means. You can also use this space to document your vision based on what you believe will happen today, this week, or in the future.

Mediate: Today, I'm meditating on...
Use this section to highlight scriptures that you would like to meditate on.

Daily Devotion
Use this space to document what God is showing you as you navigate this 40-day journey.

Thirty-Four

Day 34 - A New Altar

"For scarcely for a righteous man will one die: yet peradventure for a good man some would even dare to die. But God commendeth his love toward us, in that, while we were yet sinners, Christ died for us. Much more then, being now justified by his blood, we shall be saved from wrath through him. For if, when we were enemies, we were reconciled to God by the death of his Son, much more, being reconciled, we shall be saved by his life. And not only so, but we also joy in God through our Lord Jesus Christ, by whom we have now received the atonement." Romans 5:6-11 KJV

A New Altar

When I think of an altar, it brings me back to childhood where I would see people taking communion or kneeling and praying to God. It was always a place to me; however, as I've grown in my faith I've come to realize altars can be anything we praise or set high based on how people view it.

In Hebrew, altars were defined as a place of sacrifice. A place to offer gifts to God. In Greek, altars were considered sacred places for "gods." In Latin, altars mean "burning place" and is said to be influenced by the word altus which means "high." When you look up altars in the dictionary today, you may find a figurative meaning alluding to the fact that it's when you place someone or something up higher than another. So depending on who people believe in and pray to, that will undoubtedly dictate how and who they raise their altar to. Knowing this is important because I never considered the fact that we can erect altars in our hearts until I heard Prophetess Tiphani Montgomery mention this in a message. I haven't thought about altars the same. Primarily because people praise people as though they are gods making "sacrifices" to be like them, with them, to see them, or the like.

Going back to Romans 5, I am grateful for Christ's sacrifice. He went to the cross for you, and for me, so we wouldn't have to spend eternity in hell. Considering the turmoil we witness on earth I cannot imagine how agonizing hell would be. Let's just say, I don't want to "fool around and find out."

The enemy is crafty so he doesn't want us to be reconciled with God nor does he want us to give God praise because we know that his pride is why he lies. The enemy knows the truth and hopes that we don't.

As a result, it is important that we take stock of what we've raised as an altar in our life. If it's not God, we shouldn't be afraid to ask ourselves "why?"

"Jesus Christ the same yesterday, and to day, and for ever. Be not carried about with divers and strange doctrines. For it is a good thing that the heart be established with grace; not with meats, which have not profited them that have been occupied therein. We have an altar, whereof they have no right to eat which serve the tabernacle. For the bodies of those beasts, whose blood is brought into the sanctuary by the high priest for sin, are burned without the camp. Wherefore Jesus also, that he might sanctify the people with his own blood, suffered without the gate. Let us go forth therefore unto him without the camp, bearing his reproach. For here have we no continuing city, but we seek one to come. By him therefore let us offer the sacrifice of praise to God continually, that is, the fruit of our lips giving thanks to his name. But to do good and to communicate forget not: for with such sacrifices God is well pleased." Hebrews 13:8-16 KJV

Today, reflect on what you feel like you've made high in your life. It can be a person, place, or thing and consider that against the vastness of God. When you look at things this way, you'll quickly realize there is no comparison to God or Christ's sacrifice. Think about ways in which you see God's goodness and grace in your life. Also consider what you may need to let go of personally to get things right.

Daily Devotion (Day 34)

Gratitude: Today, I'm grateful for...
Every day is a gift! Use this space to reflect on what you are thankful for.

Dreams: I had a dream...
Use this space to document what you recall from your dreams so that you can ask the Holy Spirit to show you what it means. You can also use this space to document your vision based on what you believe will happen today, this week, or in the future.

Mediate: Today, I'm meditating on...
Use this section to highlight scriptures that you would like to meditate on.

Daily Devotion
Use this space to document what God is showing you as you navigate this 40-day journey.

Thirty-Five

Day 35 - Girded Up

> "Finally, my brethren, be strong in the Lord, and in the power of his might. Put on the whole armour of God, that ye may be able to stand against the wiles of the devil. For we wrestle not against flesh and blood, but against principalities, against powers, against the rulers of the darkness of this world, against spiritual wickedness in high places. Wherefore take unto you the whole armour of God, that ye may be able to withstand in the evil day, and having done all, to stand." Ephesians 6:10-13 KJV

Girded Up

Did you know that the word "girded" has been defined as preparing oneself for something difficult or challenging? Other common definitions or synonyms include but are not limited to surround, encircle, equip, or fasten. When we think about life, we have been put here for a purpose. Since the fall of man in Genesis, we know that the enemy has been sent down to earth, and because he is on earth, we face affliction. Let's see what Revelation 12 says about this.

"And there was war in heaven: Michael and his angels fought against the dragon; and the dragon fought and his angels, and prevailed not; neither was their place found any more in heaven. And the great dragon was cast out, that old serpent, called the Devil, and Satan, which deceiveth the whole world: he was cast out into the earth, and his angels were cast out with him. And I heard a loud voice saying in heaven, Now is come salvation, and strength, and the kingdom of our God, and the power of his Christ: for the accuser of our brethren is cast down, which accused them before our God day and night." Revelation 12:7-10 KJV

Knowing that we face an invisible enemy we have to always be on guard. Satan made a choice and has paid for it by being cast into the earth and condemned to hell. His disobedience separated him from God yet he is angry with us, God's children, because God still accepts our repentance. Whew Jesus, I just got a revelation while typing this message...

Think about a child who continually does wrong and is disobedient to their parents. This child has a sibling who strives to do everything right. The child who is disobedient will sometimes come to hate the child that is obedient because they feel like their sibling is "favored" aka the favorite. At no point are they considering their own actions are what has driven a wedge between them and their parents. This is exactly how the devil operates. He is "big mad" at God and us because of his own decision. So, his goal is to trick us into hell with him so that we won't reap the reward either.

Thank you Holy Spirit for that revelation! Revisiting Ephesians 6, it is important that we remember this:

"Finally, my brethren, be strong in the Lord, and in the power of his might. Put on the whole armour of God, that ye may be able to stand against the wiles of the devil. For we wrestle not against flesh and blood, but against principalities, against powers, against the rulers of the darkness of this world, against spiritual wickedness in high places. Wherefore take unto you the whole armour of God, that ye may be able to withstand in the evil day, and having done all, to stand. Stand therefore, having your loins girt about with truth, and having on the breastplate of righteousness; and your feet shod with the preparation of the gospel of peace; above all, taking the shield of faith, wherewith ye shall be able to quench all the fiery darts of the wicked. And take the helmet of salvation, and the sword of the Spirit, which is the word of God: praying always with all prayer and supplication in the Spirit, and watching thereunto with all perseverance and supplication for all saints; and for me, that utterance may be given unto me, that I may open my mouth boldly, to make known the mystery of the gospel, for which I am an ambassador in bonds: that therein I may speak boldly, as I ought to speak." Ephesians 6:10-20 KJV

Today, mediate on Ephesians 6 and let the Holy Spirit minister to your heart, soul, and mind.

Daily Devotion (Day 35)

Gratitude: Today, I'm grateful for...
Every day is a gift! Use this space to reflect on what you are thankful for.

Dreams: I had a dream...
Use this space to document what you recall from your dreams so that you can ask the Holy Spirit to show you what it means. You can also use this space to document your vision based on what you believe will happen today, this week, or in the future.

Mediate: Today, I'm meditating on...
Use this section to highlight scriptures that you would like to meditate on.

Daily Devotion
Use this space to document what God is showing you as you navigate this 40-day journey.

Thirty-Six

Day 36 - Built for This

"But the Lord said unto me, Say not, I am a child: for thou shalt go to all that I shall send thee, and whatsoever I command thee thou shalt speak." Jeremiah 1:7 KJV

Built for This

In Jeremiah 1, God calls him as a prophet to the nations. Verses 4-5 read:

"Then the word of the Lord came unto me, saying, Before I formed thee in the belly I knew thee; and before thou camest forth out of the womb I sanctified thee, and I ordained thee a prophet unto the nations."

Jeremiah replied:

"Then said I, Ah, Lord God! behold, I cannot speak: for I am a child." "But the Lord said unto me, Say not, I am a child: for thou shalt go to all that I shall send thee, and whatsoever I command thee thou shalt speak." Jeremiah 1:7 KJV

This reminds me of the fact that Moses was also afraid to walk in his calling because of what he thought others would think.

"And Moses said unto the Lord, O my Lord, I am not eloquent, neither heretofore, nor since thou hast spoken unto thy servant: but I am slow of speech, and of a slow tongue. And the Lord said unto him, Who hath made man's mouth? or who maketh the dumb, or deaf, or the seeing, or the blind? have not I the Lord? Now therefore go, and I will be with thy mouth, and teach thee what thou shalt say." Exodus 4:10-12 KJV

So much like Jeremiah and Moses, God has commissioned us for our call, whatever that happens to be. Often times we are looking around at others trying to compare our vine to their tree. God didn't create duplicates, he created individuals, all unique and made perfectly in His image. Don't trust me, trust God's word. "So God created man in his own image, in the image of God created he him; male and female created he them." Genesis 1:27 KJV

Knowing you were made in His image is encouraging, and allows us to be bold in our belief aka our confidence. Trusting that God is who He says He is, and we are who He says we are. Instead of focusing on what we don't have, or what we don't believe we can achieve, God is literally calling out to his children saying "just trust me!"

Ironically on Wednesday, July 31, 2024 I had a speaking engagement and I felt led to fast beforehand, asking God to give me the words to say. The morning of, I was rushing to do all the things I needed to do for work so I could drive to the location early. On my way there, I got lost which put me further behind. I also forgot my laptop because when I saw a guest in my presentation before leaving home I presumed it was the college and felt like everyone was squared away because I hadn't heard otherwise. Needless to say, upon arrival, we were scrambling to figure out how they would display my presentation because their technical expert no longer worked for them. We tried some alternative options and agreed on a plan. So, when it was time for me to speak, guess what happened??? No slides. I kept looking at the control room, hoping the slides would be displayed but when I noticed they weren't, I knew in my heart God would lead the way. And guess what He did, HE DELIVERED. My message was titled "The Power of One" and I encouraged interns, city staff, and guests to appreciate the perspective shifts from one experience, the bridges built from one relationship, and the life changes from one decision.

Today, consider what God is asking you to do, and every excuse that has been stopping you. After you write down what you believe God is calling you to do, find a scripture to encourage you. Similarly, for every excuse write down a scripture that speaks to faith over fear. I believe the Holy Spirit will minister to you in spirit and in truth. So remember, to do hard things, we must trust God too not only what we think we can do.

Daily Devotion (Day 36)

Gratitude: Today, I'm grateful for...

Every day is a gift! Use this space to reflect on what you are thankful for.

Dreams: I had a dream...

Use this space to document what you recall from your dreams so that you can ask the Holy Spirit to show you what it means. You can also use this space to document your vision based on what you believe will happen today, this week, or in the future.

Mediate: Today, I'm meditating on...
Use this section to highlight scriptures that you would like to meditate on.

Daily Devotion
Use this space to document what God is showing you as you navigate this 40-day journey.

Thirty-Seven

Day 37 - Faith for the Fight

" "And they shall fight against thee; but they shall not prevail against thee; for I am with thee, saith the Lord, to deliver thee." Jeremiah 1:19 KJV "

Faith for the Fight

On day 3, I shared my experience going through a miscarriage at the start of a global pandemic. What I knew then and still know now is that we must have faith for the fight. The battles we face aren't always natural because the enemy is out to kill, steal, and destroy destinies. When we think of the term destiny it is referring to the events or experiences one will have in the future. While we may not know the end from the beginning, there are always signs.

When I think about my life, I have been through several situations where I have seen the hand of God protect me. There was nothing I did to warrant what occurred, but God's grace was in the place. For example, I've been in two locations where I was within earshot of gunshots and literally running for my life. It was nothing but God's grace and mercy that kept me, my family, and friends safe.

Similarly, I was in a restaurant in February 2024 and we were locked in because of a fight that occurred in the nearby parking garage where there was reportedly gun fire exchanged. These situations tell me that there is a battle for our soul. In fact, I've referenced Revelation 12 multiple times because the enemy is wrought with anger since he knows that his time is short. And of course, he wants to bring some "friends" along hence the initial charm.

What I love about the scripture at the start of this chapter and the book of Jeremiah is that he had to have faith for the fight. In Jeremiah 1:19, the Word reminds us "And they shall fight against thee; but they shall not prevail against thee; for I am with thee, saith the Lord, to deliver thee." Now this was in relation to Jeremiah being called to prophesy to a nation that turned their back on God, yet God told him to be bold because he would decide how the story ended up being told. Wow, what power. Having God as your mouthpiece when the enemy hopes you'll cease.

Hebrews 11:6 tells us "But without faith it is impossible to please him: for he that cometh to God must believe that he is, and that he is a rewarder of them that diligently seek him." I'd say the fact that you made it this far shows that you are seeking a closer relationship with God and the beauty is, he wants one with you too. As you reflect on life and life experiences, think about where you are and where you want to be. What scriptures can you refer to that will help you "Fight the good fight of faith, lay hold on eternal life, whereunto thou art also called, and hast professed a good profession before many witnesses." 1 Timothy 6:12 KJV

Daily Devotion (Day 37)

Gratitude: Today, I'm grateful for...
Every day is a gift! Use this space to ree ct on what you are thankful for.

Dreams: I had a dream...
Use this space to document what you recall from your dreams so that you can ask the Holy Spirit to show you what it means. You can also use this space to document your vision based on what you believe will happen today, this week, or in the future.

Mediate: Today, I'm meditating on...
Use this section to highlight scriptures that you would like to meditate on.

Daily Devotion
Use this space to document what God is showing you as you navigate this 40-day journey.

Thirty-Eight

Day 38 - God is Great

" "For the Lord is a great God, and a great King above all " gods." Psalm 95:3 KJV

God is Great

Who do we know that can turn darkness to light?
Who can put the sun, moon, and stars in the sky?
Who has the power to open our eyes?
But God!

As I was writing this book I kept reflecting on the fact that people revere and praise people yet question God. We will quickly congratulate individuals when they achieve certain pinnacles of success yet question our creator as though He doesn't know what's best. Considering my personal life experiences I wholeheartedly believe that God is real especially considering the times and situations where God was my shield.

Every single moment of our life is a gift of grace and mercy. I am oh so grateful and I hope you are too especially when you take a step back and take stock of all that God has done for you, as well as what He has brought you through. Psalm 95 provides a good reminder regarding God's place in our earthly space.

"O come, let us sing unto the Lord: let us make a joyful noise to the rock of our salvation. Let us come before his presence with thanksgiving, and make a joyful noise unto him with psalms. For the Lord is a great God, and a great King above all gods. In his hand are the deep places of the earth: the strength of the hills is his also. The sea is his, and he made it: and his hands formed the dry land. O come, let us worship and bow down: let us kneel before the Lord our maker. For he is our God; and we are the people of his pasture, and the sheep of his hand. To day if ye will hear his voice, Harden not your heart, as in the provocation, and as in the day of temptation in the wilderness: When your fathers tempted me, proved me, and saw my work. Forty years long was I grieved with this generation, and said, It is a people that do err in their heart, and they have not known my ways: Unto whom I sware in my wrath that they should not enter into my rest." Psalm 95 KJV

Are we, in this generation, revering God in the manner in which we should? The chosen people wandered around in the wilderness for 40 years not because it was God's will but because of their hearts and the error of their ways in the sight of God. Today I encourage you to reflect on your life and any potential blind spots that God wants to reveal. After all, God cannot heal what we refuse to reveal especially considering we've been blessed with free will.

Daily Devotion (Day 38)

Gratitude: Today, I'm grateful for...

Every day is a gift! Use this space to reflect on what you are thankful for.

Dreams: I had a dream...

Use this space to document what you recall from your dreams so that you can ask the Holy Spirit to show you what it means. You can also use this space to document your vision based on what you believe will happen today, this week, or in the future.

Mediate: Today, I'm meditating on...

Use this section to highlight scriptures that you would like to meditate on.

Daily Devotion

Use this space to document what God is showing you as you navigate this 40-day journey.

Thirty-Nine

Day 39 - Pray Without Ceasing

" "And all things, whatsoever ye shall ask in prayer, believing, ye shall receive." Matthew 21:22 KJV "

Pray Without Ceasing

There is power in prayer! If prayer wasn't as powerful as it is, the enemy wouldn't try to distract us so much. As was stated in a prior chapter, the devil knows the truth, he hopes that we don't. The truth is powerful. The truth will set us free. Don't take it from me, God says what we believe shall be.

- "And all things, whatsoever ye shall ask in prayer, believing, ye shall receive." Matthew 21:22 KJV
- "Ask, and it shall be given you; seek, and ye shall find; knock, and it shall be opened unto you" Matthew 7:7 KJV
- "Be careful for nothing; but in every thing by prayer and supplication with thanksgiving let your requests be made known unto God." Philippians 4:6 KJV
- "And whatsoever ye shall ask in my name, that will I do, that the Father may be glorified in the Son. If ye shall ask any thing in my name, I will do it." John 14:13-14 KJV
- " Therefore I say unto you, What things soever ye desire, when ye pray, believe that ye receive them, and ye shall have them." Mark 11:24 KJV

When I searched the King James Version (KJV) of the bible on BibleGateway.com it returned 508 results. So if you ever need a scripture regarding prayer, search, because they are there.

Early on in my walk with God I didn't feel like I knew how to pray. I would try to emulate what I saw growing up and then I read Matthew 6.

"And when thou prayest, thou shalt not be as the hypocrites are: for they love to pray standing in the synagogues and in the corners of the streets, that they may be seen of men. Verily I say unto you, They have their reward. But thou, when thou prayest, enter into thy closet, and when thou hast shut thy door, pray to thy Father which is in secret; and thy Father which seeth in secret shall reward thee openly. But when ye pray, use not vain repetitions, as the heathen do: for they think that they shall be heard for their much speaking. Be not ye therefore like unto them: for your Father knoweth what things ye have need of, before ye ask him. After this manner therefore pray ye: Our Father which art in heaven, Hallowed be thy name. Thy kingdom come, Thy will be done in earth, as it is in heaven. Give us this day our daily bread. And forgive us our debts, as we forgive our debtors. And lead us not into temptation, but deliver us from evil: For thine is the kingdom, and the power, and the glory, for ever. Amen." Matthew 6:5-13 KJV

Learning how to pray God's way relieved a lot of the pressure I put on myself. Now I find myself praying throughout the day because regardless of what is going on around us we don't have to fear when we know God is near. That being said, we may not always be able to rely on people but we can count on God. When you face dark days remember 2 Chronicles 20:15 "for the battle is not yours, but God's." Speaking of that battle, I wrote a short poem recently that I feel led to share.

"Think it not strange when you encounter these things, the enemy is out for blood, he wants darkness to reign.

He knows his time is short so he's hoping for pain, taking young souls away withholding purpose, refrained.

He declared war from the beginning when in heaven he was sinning, got pride all up and through the church the demons think they're winning.

Believers be bold, time to stand up and fight. We know with Jesus
on our side no harm will overtake us nor plight.

Jesus died on the cross and on the third day he rose, keys to hell,
death, and the grave got Satan in a chokehold."

Today, I encourage you to pray. After all, this walk with God requires
us to have faith, to pray, and then to obey.

Gratitude: Today, I'm grateful for...
Every day is a gift! Use this space to reflect on what you are thankful for.

Dreams: I had a dream...
Use this space to document what you recall from your dreams so that you can ask the Holy Spirit to show you what it means. You can also use this space to document your vision based on what you believe will happen today, this week, or in the future.

Mediate: Today, I'm meditating on...
Use this section to highlight scriptures that you would like to meditate on.

Daily Devotion
Use this space to document what God is showing you as you navigate this 40-day journey.

Forty

Day 40 - Obey in the Promised Land

"I have fought a good fight, I have finished my course, I " have kept the faith:" 2 Timothy 4:7 KJV

Obey in the Promised Land

Congratulations, you made it to the final chapter of this devotional which is purposely titled "Obey in the Promised Land." Much like the descendants of Israel when they reached their physical "promised land" we have reached a point of reflection. We must remember when we get free, God reminds us now is the perfect time to do some work for me.

In Deuteronomy 8 verses 7-10 the land the Lord provided is described as being good land.

"...good land, a land of brooks of water, of fountains and depths that spring out of valleys and hills; a land of wheat, and barley, and vines, and fig trees, and pomegranates; a land of oil olive, and honey; a land wherein thou shalt eat bread without scarceness, thou shalt not lack any thing in it; a land whose stones are iron, and out of whose hills thou mayest dig brass. When thou hast eaten and art full, then thou shalt bless the Lord thy God for the good land which he hath given thee."

In today's society, it's easy to be excited about success. And sometimes when we reach the pinnacle of what we have been hoping and/or searching for, we forget that it was by God's grace and mercy that we have what we have, can do what we can do, and be where we are. Speaking from personal experience, when I look around and see individuals in different circumstances, I think to myself, that could've been me. Meaning having less than enough, addicted, or worse, perishing in my sin.

So we will close Day 40 with Deuteronomy 8 verses 11-20 which gives us instructions for what to do when we reach our "promised land."

"Beware that thou forget not the Lord thy God, in not keeping his commandments, and his judgments, and his statutes, which I command thee this day: lest when thou hast eaten and art full, and hast built goodly houses, and dwelt therein; and when thy herds and thy flocks multiply, and thy silver and thy gold is multiplied, and all that thou hast is multiplied; then thine heart be lifted up, and thou forget the Lord thy God, which brought thee forth out of the land of Egypt, from the house of bondage; who led thee through that great and terrible wilderness, wherein were fiery serpents, and scorpions, and drought, where there was no water; who brought thee forth water out of the rock of flint; who fed thee in the wilderness with manna, which thy fathers knew not, that he might humble thee, and that he might prove thee, to do thee good at thy latter end; and thou say in thine heart, My power and the might of mine hand hath gotten me this wealth. But thou shalt remember the Lord thy God: for it is he that giveth thee power to get wealth, that he may establish his covenant which he sware unto thy fathers, as it is this day. And it shall be, if thou do at all forget the Lord thy God, and walk after other gods, and serve them, and worship them, I testify against you this day that ye shall surely perish. As the nations which the Lord destroyeth before your face, so shall ye perish; because ye would not be obedient unto the voice of the Lord your God."

Remember, Proverbs 3 tells us "...despise not the chastening of the Lord; neither be weary of his correction: For whom the Lord loveth he correcteth; even as a father the son in whom he delighteth." As a result, we shouldn't take Deuteronomy as a rebuke but more as a reminder.

Many blessings to you as you go forth and continue running your race so that when we cross the finish line in this thing called life, we will hear well done as a result of our willingness to fight the good fight, finish our course, and keep the faith (2 Timothy 4:7).

Daily Devotion (Day 40)

Gratitude: Today, I'm grateful for...

Every day is a gift! Use this space to reflect on what you are thankful for.

Dreams: I had a dream...

Use this space to document what you recall from your dreams so that you can ask the Holy Spirit to show you what it means. You can also use this space to document your vision based on what you believe will happen today, this week, or in the future.

Mediate: Today, I'm meditating on...
Use this section to highlight scriptures that you would like to meditate on.

Daily Devotion
Use this space to document what God is showing you as you navigate this 40-day journey.

Author: Tomeria Jordan
Photographer: Patrice Boone

Tomeria Jordan is a dynamic author, speaker, and thought leader who believes everyone has a story worth sharing. With over 25 years of diverse industry experience, Tomeria brings a wealth of knowledge and expertise to her writing. Holding a master's degree in Learning and Performance Technology from the University of Maryland, Baltimore County, and a bachelor's degree in International Business and Economics from Old Dominion University, she merges academic rigor with real-world insight.

Tomeria's passion lies in inspiring individuals to embrace confidence, purpose, and faith. Through her compelling messages, she guides readers on a journey of self-discovery, healing, and restoration. Committed to helping others unlock their true potential, Tomeria Jordan empowers individuals to live with intentionality, resilience, and a deep sense of fulfillment. Visit www.tomeria.com to learn more.

Tomeria's personal goal in life is to help other people unleash their light. She currently does this through writing, podcasting, training, speaking, consulting, and social media content creation. Below are a few additional titles and resources that can be found on www.tomeria.com.

Books

- **"Live Happy, Free, and Unapologetically"**
  Virtual devotional offering a transformative experience aimed at boosting your confidence, paving the way for a life of happiness, freedom, and authenticity. In just seven days, you'll embark on a journey of self-discovery, laying the foundation for personal and professional growth. Research reveals the significant cost of lacking confidence, not only in terms of missed opportunities but also in potential earnings over a career. Therefore, understanding and embracing your identity and worth are essential in today's society. Confidence isn't a luxury—it's a necessity for living a fulfilling life.

- **S.I.N.S: Salvation Is the New Sexy - From Hot Girl to God's Girl**
  Transformative Christian self-help book that challenges societal norms and encourages readers to embrace their faith, rediscover their self-worth, and lead a purposeful life. Delving into the

origins of the word "sexy" Tomeria highlights the misconceptions around it and advocates for a shift towards prioritizing salvation over superficial values. The book offers practical advice, biblical wisdom, and personal anecdotes to help readers overcome obstacles, cultivate inner beauty, and find fulfillment through an authentic relationship with God. With powerful insights, practical tips, and thought-provoking reflection questions, this guide is perfect for anyone seeking spiritual growth and genuine happiness.

- **While You Wait - Activating Your Faith**
  The book "While You Wait - Activating Your Faith" offers a beacon of light amidst the chaos of today's world, emphasizing the importance of unwavering faith in times of uncertainty. Through its immersive week-long journey, readers are invited to discover the power within themselves, transforming moments of waiting into opportunities for personal growth and development. By embracing faith and purpose, readers can reap the rewards of resilience and emerge stronger than ever before.

- **The Non-Techie's Playbook for Podcast Success**
  Do you want to start a podcast but don't know where to start? This eBook is designed with the busybody in mind and aims to take the guesswork out of the process to save you some time.

Podcasts

Tomeria hosts and produces two podcasts, The Confidence Restored Podcast, as well as, The Perspective View Podcast.

- The **Confidence Restored Podcast by CC: America** was released in March 2020 following a month-long miscarriage. It gave Tomeria the push she needed to take the leap of faith and pursue her dreams of inspiring the lives of others through service, dedication, and faith. Ideally she wants to help others get mentally "F.I.T" and overcome any trials and tribulations they may encounter. Through personal testimonies of Faith, Inspiration, and Transformation, Tomeria and guests seek to inspire and uplift others. www.confidencerestoredpodcast.com

- **The Perspective View Podcast** is a show dedicated to discussing diversity, culture, and context beyond the boardroom. DEI today is more than a buzzword on a billboard. It is about creating safe spaces for varying perspectives, ideas, and experiences without fear of being canceled because you don't conform. The goal of creating this show is to tear down the walls of bias and build a new foundation with an open mind and understanding that the world revolves around the context of perspective. www.theperspectiveview.com

The Confidence Domain Assessment
Are you ready to unlock your full potential and boost your self-esteem? By reviewing a series of behaviors and denoting which ones resonate with you, you will gain valuable insights into your current confidence level and receive actionable steps to enhance your self-esteem. https://tomeria.mailchimpsites.com/confidencedomain

Confident Connotations LLC
Igniting meaningful conversations through lifestyle products and apparel. www.confidentconnotations.com

ACKNOWLEDGEMENTS

"GOD IS GOING TO DO IT BY HIMSELF, SO YOU WON'T QUESTION HOW IT GOT DONE. YOU WILL KNOW IT WAS GOD AND NO ONE ELSE."

JANUARY 2, 2022

The quote above was written in 2022, yet this book is a testament to that declaration. I have given God my time, talent, and treasure, and he has multiplied the words in my mouth through the work of my hand so that it may go forth and bless all those who read it.

Thank you to my Lord and Savior, Jesus Christ, and thank you to each of you for purchasing this book. I hope that "Faith Pray Obey" has touched you tremendously so that you can run your race and not get weary because God has commissioned us all to spread the gospel. Let's make God trend as we say no to sin. To accomplish this, I need your help. Please share your feedback with me at www.tomeria.com, leave a book review on whichever site is preferable to you, e.g., Amazon, Goodreads, etc. and share your thoughts and stories of faith, inspiration, and transformation via social media using the hashtag #faithprayobey.

Be blessed and keep on keeping on!

www.ingramcontent.com/pod-product-compliance
Lightning Source LLC
Chambersburg PA
CBHW071151130626
46553CB00004B/1608